Business Investment Decisions

BUSINESS INVESTMENT DECISIONS

Ian R. C. Hirst

Philip Allan

OXFORD AND NEW JERSEY

First Published 1988 by

PHILIP ALLAN PUBLISHERS LIMITED
MARKET PLACE
DEDDINGTON
OXFORD OX5 4SE (UK)

and

171 FIRST AVENUE
ATLANTIC HIGHLANDS
NEW JERSEY 07716 (USA)

British Library Cataloguing in Publication Data

Hirst, I.R.C.
    Business investment decisions.
    1. Investment. Decision making
    I. Title
    332.6

    ISBN 0-86003-549-2
    ISBN 0-86003-652-9 Pbk

Library of Congress Cataloging-in-Publication Data

Hirst, Ian R.C.
    Business investment decisions/Ian R.C. Hirst.
        p.   cm.
    ISBN 0-86003-549-2.
    ISBN 0-86003-652-9 (pbk.)
    1. Investments—Great Britain. 2. Income tax—Great Britain—Foreign income.
    3. Investments, Foreign—Taxation—Law and legislation—Great Britain.
    I. Title.
    HG5432.H57 1988
    658.1'53'0941—dc19   88-19407
                                                              CIP

Typeset at the Alden Press, London
Printed and bound in Great Britain at the Camelot Press, Southampton

Contents

Preface

This book has grown out of a series of one-day courses on project appraisal run for the Institute of Chartered Accountants in Scotland and the Chartered Institute of Management Accountants. The participants on these courses have been professionally involved in project appraisal in large UK companies, and their comments, questions and criticisms have been an important influence.

The primary audience for this book is financial managers concerned with project appraisal, and business students, particularly MBA students, at graduate or more advanced undergraduate level. The book does not attempt to disguise the difficulties and complications involved in project appraisal. It attempts to balance an awareness of the underlying principles with recommendations that are practical and workable, not merely theoretically elegant.

The book uses examples rather than algebraic derivations. It covers a broad range of situations where project appraisal techniques can be applied. It stresses such issues as tax and cash flow definition which are often passed over quickly but which raise difficult issues in practice. Although reference is made to modern theoretical developments in finance (particularly CAPM), the limitations of these methods when applied to project appraisal are also stressed.

The book assumes that readers have had a basic introduction to quantitative methods and financial concepts. Such an introduction might be provided by professional examinations, by MBA core courses, or by undergraduate courses. Elementary statistical concepts of mean, probability distribution and standard deviation are not developed from scratch. Financial concepts such as gearing, profit, depreciation etc. are also assumed.

The text aims to offer a broad coverage of topics within project appraisal, and clear exposition with numerous examples. It also aims to incorporate recent developments in the subject without losing relevance to the real world of business.

Ian Hirst
University of Edinburgh
May, 1988

1
Introduction

This book is concerned with business investment decisions. Its intention is to explain modern methods of analysing investment opportunities and to show how they can be applied in practice. Investment has a double meaning: it can mean real investment in machinery or bricks and mortar, or it can mean paper investment in shares and other securities. We are concerned with the first sort of investment decision, often called project appraisal. In this introductory chapter we shall describe the kinds of project that will be covered, the business context in which they are to be evaluated, and will explain the structure and presentation method to be used in the chapters that follow.

Projects

Most business projects take time to generate their benefits. An obvious example is the installation of new labour-saving machinery, where expenditure now brings a benefit from savings in the future. And there are many more business decisions where an outlay now will bring rewards in future years. These all fall into the same general category and can be analysed by similar techniques. Some examples are:

- A marketing campaign that will generate long-lasting brand awareness.
- Costs of legal advice and marketing research prior to launching a new financial service.
- The acquisition of another business.
- Reorganisation and redundancy costs involved in plant closures and production rationalisation.
- The purchase of new equipment rather than using it on a lease or rental basis.

Businesses

All projects need to be appraised in a business environment. Businesses, like projects, differ from each other in many respects. Most are one-person entities which use very little capital and operate on a short business cycle. Their need for professional project appraisal skills is very limited. Although the methods described in the chapters that follow have general applicability, they are particularly oriented to situations where:

- The business concerned is a public limited company (plc) domiciled in the UK with shares listed on the Stock Exchange in London.
- The company operates through subsidiaries or divisions. Investment decisions are taken at divisional level, within agreed budgets, but company headquarters makes the major financial decisions on debt, new share issues, etc.
- The projects are 'medium-sized': they are large enough to be worth careful and detailed analysis (which probably means that they involve expenditure in the tens of thousands of pounds upwards) but not so large that they require a concomitant review at headquarters level of the whole financial strategy of the company.

The text will note in a number of cases how the appraisal techniques should be modified when the context changes. There will be discussion of international investment decisions, and the Channel Tunnel example will illustrate a case where one project is, effectively, the whole company.

Sources

The ideas presented in this book have been developed, mainly in Business Schools, from the 1950s onward. In terms of their impact on the business world, they must qualify among the Business Schools' 'greatest hits'. Studies, such as those by Klammer & Walker (1984) in the US and Pike (1982) in the UK, show that the great majority of larger companies on both sides of the Atlantic now use these methods. The techniques, though, are not 'golden oldies'. There has been constant sharpening and refinement of the available techniques for investment appraisal, and this book incorporates recent thinking in the field.

The objective of this book is to give a clear, consistent, modern and practical treatment of investment decision making. It will be practical in that it will cover in detail areas such as tax and project definition which are often given scant attention in theoretical texts. It will recommend one particular approach that will be explained and justified in detail, but it is not claimed that this is the only correct approach. On matters of detail there are a number of acceptable alternative approaches and in some cases these options will be pointed out. There are also some unequivocally wrong techniques that have gained currency, and the text will also draw attention to these pitfalls.

Business Objectives

The objective of business is to create wealth, and the objective of managers in shareholder-owned businesses is to create wealth for the shareholders. This seems a bald and perhaps simplistic goal. Of course, a business works to satisfy its customers and to secure a satisfactory quality of working life for its employees. However, the relationship with customers, workers and others is a two-sided bargain, and the objective of the business in dealing with them is complex and involves both giving and getting. The business does not bargain with its shareholders: it is a vehicle for the shareholders' interests and its objective is to secure those interests.

What is it the shareholders want? Is it measured by earnings, or dividends, or capital gains? This is a difficult question and one which, at this point, we can evade. Whenever a project is found and accepted which benefits the shareholders in terms of the prospective dividends/earnings/capital gains it will produce, the shareholders will raise the value they put on their shares and the market price will rise accordingly. Setting shareholders' wealth as the objective is not an alternative to looking at future profits or dividends: it is the most appropriate method of appraising these prospective benefits. Stating the objective of maximising shareholders' wealth is simple. Working out how a particular project will affect shareholder wealth is, as the following chapters will show, no trivial matter.

One problem that investment decision makers face is, 'Do shareholders know what's good for them?' Specifically, do they respond rationally to developments in the companies that they own, or are they guilty of 'short-termism' or similar economic sins? Short-termism means that shareholders systematically undervalue benefits that will be received beyond a short (one- or two-year) horizon. When a good long-term project is launched, the immediate effect is that the company's shares may fall, even though they will rise in the longer term when the benefits start to show in the accounts. In this case there is no simple answer to the question 'Will the project increase shareholders' wealth?' In the long term it will; in the short term it won't. In the short term the share price fall may make the company liable to takeover.

This picture of short-termism should be taken with a pinch of salt. There is little doubt (none as far as the author is concerned) that shareholders genuinely want to make money from their investments and will not sell their shares at a depressed price knowingly, leaving to the purchaser a disproportionate opportunity to enjoy capital gains. In other words, if the share price falls after a long-term business investment is announced, the shareholders do not expect the effect to be reversed later. They knock down the share price, not because they systematically undervalue the long-term benefits, but because they don't agree with management's estimate of what the long-term benefits will be. Such a discrepancy is undesirable for the company. It is certainly preferable for management and shareholders to see eye to eye. Management is active; stock market investors are, normally, passive. So it is up to management to try to bridge the communication gap by explaining its policies to stockbrokers and fund managers. The gap can never be completely closed. If it opens too widely, management has lost the confidence of its shareholders and must regain it or be replaced. Our general assumption will be that discrepancies between management and shareholder appraisals are small, temporary, and without any systematic effect on the appraisal process. The later chapters on quantitative appraisal techniques will ignore them.

The Big Picture — An Overview of the Appraisal Process

King (1975) has proposed a six-stage process for project appraisal. All of these stages are important, even though one of them, evaluation, lends itself more than the others to sophisticated quantitative analysis. The six stages are:

(1) *Search* The whole investment process is initiated by spotting a promising opportunity. Profit-making ideas are not easy to come by. There is keen competition for them, and only those who look diligently are likely to be successful.

(2) *Screening* At this stage the feasibility of the project will be reviewed. It is also at this stage that issues of strategic fit can be considered, although this may be done at a later stage.

(3) *Definition* It is a long step from a basic written description of a project to a detailed identification of what the project would involve. Costs and revenues are certainly part of this process, but there is also office/factory space to be found as well as suitable personnel. Market research or other investigation may be needed. There may well be a number of different ways in which the basic idea for a project could be exploited, and it is important at the definition stage to generate some alternative possibilities for further analysis.

(4) *Evaluation* The bulk of this book will be concerned with this stage. There are a variety of techniques, some of them quite sophisticated, which are available. The objective of evaluation is to put forward a full package of information about the project, both numerical and

descriptive, that will assist the final decision. Evaluation rarely ends with a single number.

(5) *Decision* This uses the package of information produced at the evaluation stage and may return to consider strategic issues. The intention will be to look at the project from all aspects: the returns, the risks, the unquantifiable advantages and disadvantages. The result is a 'yes', a 'no', or perhaps a reference back for further study along specified lines.

(6) *Post-acceptance analysis* A company is wise to learn from experience, and post-acceptance analysis formalises the process. The main lessons to be learned will be about bias, particularly over-optimism in forecasting benefits and underestimating costs. These lessons can be fed back into the appraisal system.

The chapters that follow will have very little to say about the first two stages. This may seem surprising: generating good investment ideas is, after all, the essential foundation on which the long-run future of any business is built; no amount of sophisticated analysis can save a company that is not coming up with good projects to appraise. The fact is, though, that finding business ideas requires originality and creativity, usually based on detailed, specific experience of the markets and/or technology involved. There is little useful generalisation that can be done, and it tends to sound platitudinous. Two very important points are:

(1) The organisation of the business must recognise that generating investment projects is an essential ingredient for success. Resources must be allocated to the task. A management team that devotes all its energies to managing today's business is neglecting its responsibility to develop tomorrow's. To use a nautical metaphor, members of senior management need to be continuously on watch, scanning the horizon for any threats or opportunities that may arise. The present tendency is to avoid concentrating the responsibility for investment search on a small team of planners at head office. It should be part of the management function throughout the company. Those closest to the operational front line are often in the best position to spot opportunities. One objective of human resource management within the company will be to motivate staff to initiate investment proposals and to put them into channels for further appraisal. This will involve rewarding, probably in monetary ways, those whose ideas are adopted, and turning down other ideas without offending their proposers.

(2) The objective is to find projects that are a good fit for the talents and resources of the business. Much time and effort can be saved if the business has a sense of strategic direction and knows what it is

looking for in a project. A company that has identified its own
territory, its area of competitive advantage, will be in a much better
position to appraise projects realistically based on experience. It will
be in a much better position to build a business made up of a group
of projects which tend to support each other through marketing and
technological cross-linkages. There is a large and useful literature on
business strategy formulation, but it falls outside the scope of this
text. A great many projects involving choice of production techniques
etc. will not involve strategic issues. And, similarly, there are many
aspects of strategy formulation that are not concerned with project
appraisal.

Contents

Chapter 2 is concerned with the third of King's stages, project definition.
It asks 'What do we need to know about a project before we can start to
appraise it?' The questions, of course, are usually answered by the engineers,
salesmen or senior managers who are proposing the project. The skills that
they use in answering them may involve engineering calculations, marketing
research or other specialist techniques. Our concern is with asking the right
questions about a proposed project and then making good use of the
answers.

Project definition is often passed over quickly as authors and lecturers
move on to quantitative methods. Those who do project appraisals in the
real world soon find that defining a project throws up a host of difficult
issues. How are overheads, working capital changes, interest payments, etc.
to be treated? The chapter tries to cover the wide variety of items that arise
in practice.

Chapter 4 on the tax regime is also relevant to the process of project
definition, since the tax effects of any project must be identified before
analysis can begin. Another aspect of project definition is consideration of
risk. The information required for project risk analysis is covered in Chapter
8.

Chapters 3, 5, 6 and 7 are all concerned with different aspects of
evaluation. This may not be the most important of King's stages, but is the
one where formal quantitative techniques can be used. It is a large part of
the purpose of this text to explain these techniques.

Chapter 3 is concerned with the basic types of appraisal calculation,
particularly Net Present Value (NPV) and Internal Rate of Return (IRR).
It shows how these can be calculated and why they are superior to other
traditional methods. It also explains the limitations of the techniques and
the circumstances in which they can be misleading. It discusses the proper
allowance for inflation in appraisal calculations. Inflation is often a controversial issue when appraisal methods are used in practice.

Chapter 5 discusses the rate of return which a business should require on its projects. Two approaches (the Dividend–Growth Model and the Capital Asset Pricing Model) are covered in the main text. Two other methods are covered in appendices. This abundance of choice does not mean that the question of setting a required rate of return is one on which the literature has made particularly impressive progress. On the contrary, it is an area where it has proved particularly difficult to find methods that are right in theory and workable in practice. Several different ways of trying to reconcile these two requirements are explained. In many cases, the different methods will give rather similar results.

Chapters 6 and 7 are concerned with special types of project appraisal where specialised techniques can be used. Chapter 6 is concerned with the evaluation of leases as an alternative to purchase with or without borrowed funds. Leasing is a financial decision and thus makes an important difference to the appraisal method. The tax treatment of leases is, of course, also important. Chapter 7 is largely concerned with decisions to scrap old equipment, to replace old equipment with new, and when to switch from older to newer technology. There are specific methods of analysis that can be used in these cases.

Chapter 8 covers risk analysis. Formal risk analysis has not been very common in the past. It is now becoming more popular, partly because the calculations are made much easier by using spreadsheet packages on personal computers. The chapter explains in some detail how a PC can be used for this purpose.

Finally, Chapter 9 looks at appraisal systems in practice. How well do they work in an organisational context? What are the recent criticisms of the established appraisal techniques?

Presentation

All the calculations involved in project appraisal can be made much more easily and accurately on a computer than by hand. The chapters that follow, however, explain how to do the sums manually. In most cases it will be clear to anyone who has experimented with a spreadsheet package on a PC how the calculations can be transferred from paper to monitor. Risk analysis is the exceptional case where the use of a spreadsheet is described explicitly.

The methods of analysis discussed throughout the book are almost all illustrated by examples. The generous use of examples has the disadvantage of slowing down and interrupting the explanation of the underlying theory. However, in the author's view examples are the clearest way of explaining any technique and that is why they take up so much of the text. Many of the examples, though, are greatly simplified versions of the problems that arise in practice. The traditional author's licence has been used in several ways. For instance, the examples treat the costs and benefits of projects as annual amounts. In practice, most businesses look at the inflows and outflows on a monthly basis. Doing this in the text would produce twelve times as many numbers, make the tables harder to read and introduce no new concepts, so annual numbers have been used.

The text also goes into considerable detail on the UK tax system and how taxes come into the appraisal system. However, when an example is being used to illustrate a quite different point, we have not hesitated to leave tax out completely. Some examples in the text are extended ones. In many cases, though, the text treats the issues one at a time. It is left to the practitioner to juggle them all at once.

References and Further Reading

King, P. (1975) 'Is the emphasis of capital budgeting theory misplaced?', *Journal of Business Finance and Accounting*, Vol. 12, No. 1, pp. 68–82.

Klammer, T.P. and Walker, M.C. (1984) 'The continuing increase in the use of sophisticated capital budgeting techniques', *California Management Review*, Fall, Vol. 27, No. 1, pp. 137–48.

Pike, R.H. and Wolfe, M.B. (1987) *A Review of Capital Investment Trends in Large Companies*, University of Bradford Management Centre, Occasional Paper No. 8701/8702.

2

Project Definition

Introduction

An investment idea starts as a concept: as the idea that a new market might profitably be served, or that it might be beneficial to introduce a newly-invented technology. The systematic search for original ideas is a vital area of business management, but one that is largely outside the scope of this book except for a brief discussion in Chapter 8. The next stage is to move from a concept to a specific project that can be appraised and then accepted or rejected.

It is often asserted that projects should be analysed on the *incremental cash-flow* on an *after-tax* basis that they offer. This chapter will explain why projects should be measured in this way. The concepts are clear enough in theory, but there are several difficult issues which emerge when it comes to applying them to actual projects. The chapter will look at each concept in turn, explain the problems, and recommend how it can be applied in practice. In this chapter we only consider the general principles involved in incorporating the tax system into the analysis. Taxation is a very important aspect of project appraisal, and Chapter 4 will look in detail at the UK system and its impact on project appraisal. It will also consider the analysis of investments overseas.

Incrementality

Every project represents a choice. It is either accepted or rejected, and the project is defined in cash flow terms as the *difference* between these alternatives. This means that the analyst must consider in equal detail the consequences of proceeding with the project or not proceeding. Consider expenditure at a chemical factory that is needed to comply with new health and safety regulations. It is sometimes said that such an investment is unanalysable, because it brings in no extra revenue. Looked at from an incremental viewpoint, this is not so. If the investment is not made, the plant must be closed down. All the revenues are incremental, and the investment, properly appraised, may well turn out to be highly profitable.

Every project must be compared with an alternative — but what alternative? The short answer is that, to be accepted, a project should be more attractive than every possible alternative. If there is only one, there is no problem. But there may easily be several. In this case one of the alternatives must be chosen as a 'base-case' and all the others measured against it. The one which measures most highly on the chosen appraisal system is the best alternative so long as the appraisal system is transitive. Transitivity means that, if A scores more highly than B when they are both measured relative to a 'base case' alternative C, A would also be the winner if it were measured directly relative to B. Transitivity is a desirable property in an appraisal system. The methods recommended later are transitive. They avoid the need to consider the incremental cash flows generated by all possible pairings.

To work the project appraisal system efficiently it is necessary to make sure that new projects are matched against the best available alternatives, even when those alternatives involve unwelcome fundamental changes in the business. Any project can look good if it is paired against a sufficiently poor opponent. There is a real risk that an appraisal system can busy itself with the analysis of small-scale changes and that opportunities for major restructuring never get a look in. It is management's job to make sure that does not happen.

The Cash Flow Rule

It is a natural instinct for businessmen to think in accounting terms and to measure projects in terms of the profit they will produce. It is a natural instinct but, for our purposes, it is incorrect. Reported profit is a number presented by directors and managers (insiders) to shareholders, bankers and others (outsiders). It is therefore a number which has been manipulated so as to give outsiders a simplified and comprehensible picture of the company's affairs. To give one example: expenses are not deducted at the time they are incurred, but are held back (or brought forward) so that they can be offset against the revenues they will produce. This manipulation makes sense when the objective is communication with outsiders. It does not make sense when management is doing its own internal analysis. From the management viewpoint, and ultimately from the shareholders' viewpoint too, the key financial measure is cash flow. These are the raw numbers from which other indicators of financial achievement are derived. For project appraisal, we want to start with the basic data, not with numbers that have been modified and adjusted with some other purpose in mind, and we therefore work with incremental cash flows.

The cash flow rule needs to be applied with care and common sense. The objective is to boil down the whole project to a series of cash flows that will occur on specific dates in the future. Sometimes this is impractical. Consider two examples:

(a) A project involves building on land that the company already owns adjacent to the existing factory. If the project goes ahead, no cash will change hands for the land. If the project does not go ahead, the land will not be sold because the company expects to expand eventually and believes it is most efficient to have its operations close together.

(b) A company measures the amount of direct labour that would be required for a project, and the cost of that labour. It also reckons that it spends £2.00 on employing managers and other indirect staff (personnel, property management and maintenance, etc.) for every £10.00 it spends on direct labour. If the project is accepted, however, there would be no immediate plan to hire more indirect staff.

In these two cases, there seem to be no out-of-pocket expenses involved in acquiring the land or paying for indirect labour. But this would be a narrow and rather superficial view. In the first example the land that the project uses is a valuable resource, and the project should be charged for using it. If the project goes ahead, there will eventually be cash flow implications, because some subsequent desirable project will not fit on the land the company owns and a new site will have to be acquired. The timing and amount of this cash item, though, is highly uncertain.

Looking at it another way, the company has spare land now because when it originally bought the site, it bought more than it needed. On a narrow cash flow interpretation, the whole of the site would be charged to the first development there, even though it did not use all the land.

In the second example, the basic fact is that the new project will surely put an additional burden on the management and support services of the company, and this will involve costs that should properly be charged against the project. The problem is that the link between taking on new projects and taking on new indirect staff is likely to be a loose one. Some projects can proceed without hiring more indirect staff; some indirect staff will be hired without the decision being specifically linked to any project.

In both these examples, it makes sense to include 'allowances' in the project cash flows which do not correspond to specific cash disbursements or receipts. By doing this, we are not really going against the spirit of the cash flow rule. If we could conveniently match up projects with land purchases and additional indirect staff costs, we would do it. But we have inadequate information and must therefore use an approximate method.

The effort to define projects in cash flow terms is a laudable goal, but it can only be taken so far.

We now consider more specifically how different items enter into the cash flow analysis.

Working Capital

It is easy to identify an investment with a new fixed asset that will be acquired. In fact, industry has roughly as much of its capital employed in working capital as in fixed assets, so projects will often require as much money to be committed in raw materials, stock of finished goods and debtors as in plant and buildings. If the amount owed on an interest-free basis to creditors rises as a result of the project, this can be offset against the other items. Working capital has two special features as a component of project cash flows. First, it is usually recovered at the end of the project as the last items of stock are sold and the final customers pay their bills. Second, increases in working capital, unlike most project related expenditures, are not at present tax-deductible.

Depreciation and Writing-Down Allowances

Depreciation is not a cash item. It is, under normal accounting procedures, an allocation of historical cost. Since the whole of the initial amount spent on fixed assets is recorded as a cash flow when it is incurred, later subtraction of depreciation would be double counting. Depreciation for financial reporting purposes is therefore strictly irrelevant in project appraisal. Neither are writing-down allowances an element of cash flow, although they are not irrelevant because they do affect the amount and timing of tax payments. Taxes are a cash item which we shall consider in detail later.

Overheads

Overheads arise from costs that cannot be readily allocated to the segments (projects, departments, etc.) of the business. As such they fall into two categories:

(1) Costs which are not linked in any way to the level of activity within the different segments. Pure examples of this are hard to find. The cost of writing a computer program to handle the company's personnel records might be an example. Once the program is written it can serve any number of staff without further expenditure. The business needs

to cover expenses of this type before it can be called profitable, but the expenditure cannot be linked to the separate revenue-generating parts of the firm. In an economist's sense, the cost of the program is a fixed cost, and project appraisal is only concerned with variable costs in the sense that they vary depending on whether the project is accepted or not. This type of overhead should not be included in cash flow.

(2) Costs which are linked to individual projects in such a complicated way that it is impractical to allocate them accurately or precisely and some rough and ready method must be used instead. Most firms will have systems which allocate the costs of heating and lighting, general management, personnel, etc. to the separate revenue-generating parts of the firm. These allocations cannot be accurate, but they are approximations to genuine incremental costs. Accepting a project will impose an extra burden on general management, personnel, etc. As long as the overhead allocation is an honest best-guess at what these incremental costs will be, they should be included in the project cash flows.

Our objective in applying the incremental approach to the measurement of cash flow is to capture as fully as possible the consequences of accepting the project. This means identifying all the knock-on effects and trying to quantify them. Do not forget the installation and set-up costs of new equipment, costs of staff recruitment and training, the negative effect on sales of existing products if the project puts a new item into the product range. All these items, and many others, may need to be included in a full assessment of incremental cash flow.

The Cash Flow Measurement Boundary

The diagram in Figure 2.1 shows the flow of cash from the project into the pockets of investors. The liability for corporate tax has been split into two parts. In most tax systems, interest on company borrowings is deducted before the figure for taxable income is struck. The final tax paid can therefore be divided into two parts: the tax that would have been payable if the company had no interest to deduct, *less* the amount of the interest, times the marginal tax rate.

The diagram shows that 'project cash flow' is a hopelessly ill-defined term. Cash flow to what entity? After what deductions? There are two main problem areas. One is taxation, which is considered in detail shortly. The other is financial flows.

Suppose a company is thinking of investing in a new £50,000 item of equipment. If it goes ahead, it will get £40,000 of the money in the form of a bank loan. How much is the initial cash outlay, £10,000 or £50,000?

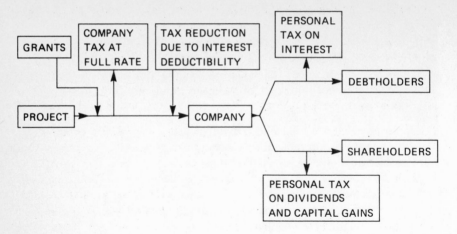

Figure 2.1

First, notice that whatever we decide, we must be consistent. If we take the outflow as £10,000, we must measure cash inflows after interest and loan repayments have been deducted. In this case we would be measuring cash flows from and to the shareholders. If we take the company as the entity, then £50,000 is the outflow and the costs of servicing the loan would not be deducted. This would still be the case, of course, if the dealer who sold the equipment provided the loan rather than a bank.

We would also have to change our appraisal standards depending on which cash flow we measured. The company as an entity would accept all the risk and receive all the return (after company tax) from the investment. The shareholder would accept all the risk but would not receive all the return, because some return goes to the debtholders. The appraisal of the cash flows would have to be different in the two cases to reflect this. The shareholders would require a higher rate of return on their investment to compensate for the greater proportionate risk. With these qualifications a valid cash flow could be measured at either the company or the shareholder level. It might seem from our emphasis on the creation of shareholder wealth as the fundamental company objective that cash flow to shareholders should be the measure. In fact, most businesses prefer to take the company as the entity, and we shall generally follow this preference. The advantage of this is that the project decision can be made independently of the financing decision. Investment appraisal is usually carried out at division or subsidiary level. Financing is a head office function. It is therefore administratively much more convenient to make investment decisions separately from financing decisions. This requires that cash-flow measurement should be measured without making any adjustment for financing cash flows.

In practice, the nature of the UK tax system means that it is usually impossible to make good investment decisions without some consideration of the financing aspects. And there are some situations where cash flows must logically be measured to and from the shareholders. The main example would be lease or buy/borrow decisions, where the choice is between two methods of finance, and financing cash flows cannot be ignored. We consider this important case in detail in Chapter 6. But our general rule is that financing flows are ignored when project cash flow is measured.

Taxes and Cash Flows — Principles

The detailed impact of the UK tax system is covered in a later chapter. Here we are concerned with the principles according to which cash flows must be adjusted to take account of taxes.

Our guiding principle is to select projects that will contribute to shareholder wealth. To do this we need to measure the cash flows that contribute to shareholder wealth, and wealth is to be measured in terms of the market value of the shareholdings. The question is how tax should be treated in calculating these cash flows, remembering that there are two levels of tax that may be relevant, company tax and personal tax.

We can illustrate this problem with an example. Consider two companies, A and B, both of which are debt-free and pay out all their earnings as dividends. A pays company tax at a rate of 35 per cent, but B has unused tax allowances that ensure it will not pay for the current year or in the foreseeable future. We also suppose that A has shareholders who are private individuals paying tax on their dividend income at 60 per cent. The shares of B are held by charitable trusts which pay no income tax. Finally, suppose that both companies will earn 50p per share this year and every future year. How will the marketable wealth represented by a share in A compare with that for a share in B?

	A	B
Pre-tax earnings per share	50.0p	50.0p
After-corporate tax earnings per share	32.5p	50.0p
After-corporate and personal tax income per share	13.0p	50.0p

The stock market will not value these shares equally, even though they have the same pre-tax earnings per share. The fact that B doesn't have to pay company tax makes it more valuable to investors. Conversely, the market will not value B's shares at 3.8 times as much as A's even though its shareholders are receiving 3.8 times as much in their pockets after all tax has been paid. If the trusts were to sell their shares in B they could not pass on their tax privileges to the purchaser. The price that they or any other shareholder could get would be independent of their own tax position.

It follows, then, that marketable wealth will be based on cash flows after company tax but before shareholder tax. Company B's shares will be worth 1.54 ($= 50.0/32.5$) times as much as A's.

Tax Deductibility of Interest

It is, unfortunately, impossible to define cash flow in a way that is independent of the associated finance and which deducts company tax. Because interest payments are tax deductible, the amount of extra company tax that a project generates will depend on how much debt is used in the financing. This creates a dilemma because two of our principles are in conflict. It is natural to assume that companies know what is good for them when it comes to financing decisions, and that they will not employ one source of finance if another, cheaper, source is available. If debt has tax advantages over equity, surely companies will make the maximum possible use of debt and the minimum use of equity. There is no evidence that companies actually behave in this way. Most large companies would clearly be welcomed at the banks or in the corporate bond markets if they decided to borrow more. Companies must limit their use of debt and its associated tax benefits for one of two reasons:

(1) Management caution   Increased use of debt makes it more likely that the company will go bankrupt or will find itself in the danger zone where bankruptcy becomes a real possibility and evasive action has to be taken. Shareholders may be willing to run this risk. No doubt their investments are diversified so that the failure of a single company is not a disaster, and they will reap the benefits of the tax savings that debt will create. From management's point of view the balance of advantage may look different. Bankruptcy, forced merger or distress sale of divisions of the company may cause incumbent management to lose its jobs with serious consequences for its future potential earnings. Management gets no direct benefit from company tax savings. As a result, management may have a preference for equity over debt finance even when debt is cheaper, and may have the power to impose an inefficient capital structure on the firm. According to this model, there is nothing implausible about a project appraisal method which shows a project to be more attractive the more debt is used — even though the project is actually going to be financed with only a limited use of debt.

(2) Failure to incorporate the wider impact of the tax system At the company tax level, debt clearly has an advantage over equity. But the providers of finance are interested in minimising their overall tax burden — company tax and the subsequent personal taxes that they pay. Perhaps equity finance has advantages at the personal tax level that offset its company tax disadvantage. This would explain why so many companies use only modest amounts of debt in their financial structures. It would also imply that our project appraisal methods should be neutral with respect to project financing. A project should not appear either more or less attractive depending on the amount of debt it uses. Is there any reason to believe that the personal tax system acts to counteract the bias towards debt in company tax?

The argument in favour has been produced by Miller (1977). It is illustrated in Figure 2.2, which shows the two routes by which a company can give a return to investors and shows the tax bite along each route. Writing about the US system of the time, Miller pointed out that interest income would escape company tax but would be subject to the full bite of personal income tax. The returns from equity would be taxed at company level, but would then give the shareholders a return made up partly of dividends and partly of capital gains. Historically, capital gains have been the larger element. Miller argued that the tax bite on both these forms of income would be, in practice, very low. Capital Gains Tax rates have usually been lower than income tax rates. Moreover, CGT is only payable when securities are sold and this enables payments to be postponed. A tax postponed is a tax alleviated. Finally, investors can offset capital losses against gains for tax purposes and show ingenuity in timing the losses to give the greatest possible benefit.

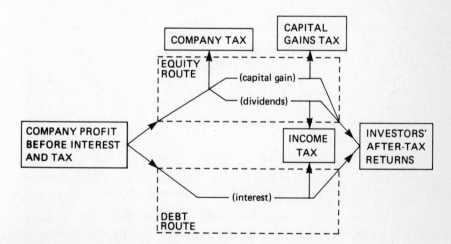

Figure 2.2

As far as dividends are concerned, US investors have been able to buy shares on margin (i.e. borrowing part of the purchase price) and to offset the interest against the dividends for tax purposes. Since dividend yields are typically low compared to interest rates, this enables them to wash out the liability for income tax on dividends, too.

In Miller's model, equilibrium is reached when all investors for whom debt is more tax efficient than equity hold debt, and those for whom equity is more efficient hold equity. At the margin, debt and equity are equally tax efficient, and a project appraisal system independent of the form of finance used would be justified.

The UK tax system is different and the loopholes gape less widely, but it would still be possible to hypothesise a tax-equilibrium model like Miller's.

Unfortunately, there is no clear empirical evidence that enables us to choose between these two models, but the absence of strong clientele effects (investors choosing the type of security they will buy based on their tax status) tends to argue against the Miller model. UK financial markets are now dominated by pension funds and other tax-exempt investors, and from their point of view the current UK system tends to discriminate in favour of payout (either interest or dividends) and against retentions. In the chapters that follow, we shall take the tax system at face value and measure cash flows after company tax, with company tax being calculated in a way that allows for interest deductibility. The Miller arguments, though, serve as a warning that the tax regime is really a complex, integrated system, and our method probably involves some over-simplification and inaccuracy.

Summary

We have argued in this chapter that:

(1) Cash flows should be measured at company, not shareholder, level. Financing cash flows are not included. A bank loan to finance a project does not count as a cash inflow and the subsequent service payments are not cash outflows.

(2) Cash flows should be measured after company tax but before personal tax.

(3) Company tax should be calculated realistically. This means that forecast tax payments should be reduced to allow for the tax deductibility of interest on loans justified by the debt capacity of the project.

This chapter has been concerned with the principles of cashflow measurement. The example that follows illustrates these principles, but is based on a simplified tax system. It does not correspond to the current UK system which is covered in detail in Chapter 4.

An Example

Goldspar is a successful and expanding manufacturer of yacht equipment. Masts and spars are its largest product, but winches are another important line. New technology is influencing winch manufacture. At present Goldspar machines the internal working parts of its winches from solid aluminium. Rival manufacturers, however, are using parts made by sintering metal powder into moulds. This is potentially a cheaper production method. Although the market price of winches has not been affected so far, Goldspar management expects them to fall by 5 per cent in two years' time.

Goldspar is considering adopting the new technology. Unfortunately, it invested five years ago in new lathes which would not be needed for the new manufacturing process. Information about the old and new equipment is as follows.

The old equipment was bought for £158,000 and has received a 25 per cent writing down allowance for each year. Its book value is now £37,500, but its market value is estimated to be £42,000. Its potential useful life is reckoned to be a further 10 years, and the value if sold at that time would be about £8,000.

The new machine would cost £70,000, and the dealer is offering 90 per cent finance for five years at 13 per cent interest. Goldspar also pays 13 per cent on its overdraft. Goldspar can either pay £70,000 cash, or £7,000 down and £17,912 at the end of each year for the next five years. The equipment would be likely to last 10 years. The moulds would be unsaleable and would be scrapped, but the other equipment could be sold for £5,000. The benefit from the new machine comes from the lower materials costs. At current output levels, the new system would save £4,000 per annum in raw materials costs. In addition, the company now has £10,000 tied up in a large stock of the various aluminium sections from which the components are machined. This would be replaced by a stock of sintering powder worth only £1,000. The inventory of aluminium sections takes up 1,500 square feet of factory space. The new manufacturing system would require only 500 square feet. All the space in the factory is currently being used and Goldspar is planning to extend the factory in two or three years' time. Expected output, labour and energy requirements are the same for both manufacturing methods.

The company estimates that overheads (all items except direct labour and materials) add 80 per cent on top of direct costs. This overhead covers all management functions, including marketing, and the costs of the firm's

30,000 square foot factory/office building. The cost of the building (rent, rates, heat, light etc.) are reckoned at £3.50 per square foot.

Goldspar pays tax at 35 per cent with a one-year lag in the tax payment system. Goldspar's financial policy is to finance 50 per cent of its working capital requirements through a bank loan, and 25 per cent of its fixed capital requirements.

Calculate the incremental after-tax cash flow for this investment project.

Answer

First, notice that some of the information is irrelevant. The expected fall in winch prices does not affect the decision. It will have the same effect on revenue whichever manufacturing technique Goldspar chooses. The offer of finance by the dealer is also a red herring. The offer does not involve a hidden subsidy (which should not be ignored), and we do not want to include financing items in cash flow. We treat the £70,000 cost as a cash item and assume that the incremental borrowing follows the company's normal policy whether or not the dealer's finance offer is accepted.

There is no incremental revenue from the project. The major items of savings are:

(a) Materials costs £5,000 per annum

(b) Overheads We should not assume that saving £5,000 in direct costs will save a further 80 per cent × £5,000 = £4,000 in overhead costs. We need to look specifically at the overhead items and decide whether they will be affected. In this case there is no reason to suppose management and marketing expenses will fall, but the new technology would release 1,000 square feet of space. In the short run this space might lie idle, but Goldspar is expanding and it would not stay vacant long. Strictly the incremental cash flow implication is that, with new technology, the need to build a factory extension will be marginally postponed. In practice the use of an overhead charge for space seems a more practical alternative way of making the calculation. This gives a saving of 3.50 × 1,000 = £3,500 per annum, and we treat this as a taxable inflow.

(c) Working capital When the new technology is installed it saves £9,000 in raw materials stock. This is a once-for-all, non-taxable cash inflow. At the end of the project in 10 years' time the old technology would give

back (£9,000) more than the new. So there is an incremental, non-taxable cash flow of (£9,000) at the end.

(d) Capital costs The immediate cash outflow associated with the project is £70,000 − £42,000 = £28,000. At the end of the project, there will be £8,000 − £5,000 = £3,000 *less* coming in as scrap value from the new project compared with the alternative.

(e) Interest Throughout the life of the project there will be £9,000 less in raw materials stock and this will reduce borrowing by £4,500 and annual interest by £585. We must also consider the borrowing related to fixed assets. The incremental value of borrowing associated with the fixed asset will be 25 per cent of the incremental book value of the assets in each year. In the first year the incremental interest will be 28,000 × 0.25 × 0.13 = £910. The 'incremental asset' of £28,000 will be reduced by the writing down allowance of 25 per cent each year.

Tax is payable on the cash savings, less the incremental Writing Down Allowance and the incremental interest. A curious feature of the WDA system is that the tax consequences of a project continue to dribble on long after the project has ended. In this example, we cut off the incremental cash flows after 11 years, and make a rough adjustment to allow for the fact that we are bringing some small, residual tax payments forward. In fact, incremental WDA would be £526 in the 10th year, £1,145 in the 11th (an increase because of the scrap value adjustments), £858 in the 12th, and so on. To bring the calculations to a halt, we replace these elements with a single writing down allowance of £4,000 in the 10th year. The sum of the allowances in the 11th and subsequent years is £4,580. The benefits of these allowances will be delayed. As a rough approximation, we take 75% of this sum and treat it as an allowance available now. Adding this to £526 gives, approximately, £4,000. In the same way, the interest allowance for fixed assets in the 10th year of £500 is an estimated equivalent at that time of a

Table 2.1 Cash Flow Calculation — Goldspar Example (£)

	Now	yr 1	yr 2	yr 3	yr 4	yr 5	yr 6	yr 7	yr 8	yr 9	yr 10	yr 11
(1) Capital outlay	(28000)											
(2) Materials saving		4000	4000	4000	4000	4000	4000	4000	4000	4000	4000	
(3) Space saving		3500	3500	3500	3500	3500	3500	3500	3500	3500	3500	
(4) Depreciation		7000	5250	3937	2953	2215	1661	1246	934	701	4000	
(5) Working capital	9000										(9000)	
(6) Interest on working capital loan @ 13%		(585)	(585)	(585)	(585)	(585)	(585)	(585)	(585)	(585)	(585)	
(7) Interest on fixed asset loan @ 13%		910	683	512	384	288	216	162	121	91	500	
(8) Taxable income (2) + (3) − (4) − (6) − (7)		175	2152	3636	4748	5582	6208	6677	7030	7293	3585	
(9) Tax @ 35%			61	753	1273	1662	1954	2173	2337	2461	2553	1255
(10) Net cash flow (1) + (2) + (3) + (5) − (9)	(19000)	7500	6439	6747	6227	5838	5546	5327	5163	5039	(7053)	(1255)

long tail of incremental interest allowances stretching indefinitely into the future. Table 2.1 shows the cash flow calculation in this example. The investment is assumed to take place at the beginning of a tax year.

Study Questions

1. Swallow plc manufactures luxury cars. It is considering producing a convertible version of its most popular model. It believes that it could sell 3,000 convertibles per year, and that none of these sales would be at the expense of existing models. The details of the project are as follows:

    (a) It would take two years to get convertibles into dealers' showrooms. In the first year the costs (mainly design) would be £7 million. In the second year the costs (some design, but mainly tooling up) would be £28 million.
    (b) If the project does not go ahead there will be redundancies costing £1.5 million in the design office. If the project does go ahead there will be no redundancies because the design staff will have work to do on new models when it ends. The project will terminate six years from now (that is, after four years of sales) when the basic model on which the convertible is based goes out of production.
    (c) The convertible will be backed by its own marketing and sales budget of £1.5 million for each year in which the new product will be on sale.
    (d) There is sufficient production capacity on Swallow's existing assembly lines for the new convertible. No modification to the line is needed and the convertibles will be produced by using the assembly line for extra hours. Additional direct labour will be needed, and assembly line workers will be recruited accordingly.
    (e) For each convertible the revenue to the manufacturer will be £13,500.

    The costs associated with each car are as follows:

Bought-in parts and materials	£4,200
Labour costs (direct manual labour)	£2,600

    Assume that cars are sold, and the production costs are incurred, immediately the car is produced.
    The company's internal accounting system also allocates the following indirect costs to each car.

Management and administrative overheads	£500
Space (building and maintenance)	£800
Depreciation of assembly line installation costs	£1,000
Heat, light and power for manufacturing operations	£300

    Swallow has sufficient tax allowances so that it pays no corporation tax. Assume all figures are subject to zero inflation.
    Calculate the incremental cash flow for the convertible project.

2. A medium-sized financial services company currently occupies rented office accommodation in central London. It signed a lease agreement seven years ago which still has eight years to run. The company believes that, at the end of this lease, communications technology will have developed to the point where it will be able to move its whole head office operation out of London. In the meantime its business is expanding and it needs more space. The company is considering two alternatives:

(a) To rent additional office accommodation at a cost of £375,000 for the first year, rising by 5 per cent per year.

(b) To purchase a small freestanding office block in outer London. The price would be £11 million. A mortgage of £9 million would be taken out on the property. Interest at 9 per cent would be paid on this amount each year, but no repayment of the principal amount would be required. The building would be sold and the mortgage repaid at the end of eight years. It is expected that the value of the property would appreciate at 8 per cent per annum over the period. There are no writing down allowances associated with the ownership of commercial buildings. Any gain on the disposal of the building would be subject to corporation tax.

The company pays corporation tax at a rate of 35 per cent with a lag of one year. What is the incremental after-tax cash flow from buying an office building rather than renting?

3. Mephistos plc makes household electrical goods and is considering adding a toaster to its range. The company will only be able to compete in this market by setting up a sophisticated automated production line. The details of the project are as follows:

(a) Sales will start one year after the instigation of the project. The costs during the first year will be:
  (i) Purchase of factory — £800,000
  (ii) Purchase of manufacturing equipment — £2.1 million
  (iii) Design and set-up and employee retraining costs — £700,000

(b) The design potential of the factory will be 1.25 million toasters per year. It is expected that the achieved sales levels will make it possible to operate the factory at 80 per cent of this capacity. The product will become outdated and the project will terminate after 10 years of production and sales.

(c) Average revenue per toaster will be £11.50. This figure will not increase over time.

(d) The toaster factory will be an autonomous business unit under its own managing director. The annual costs and other charges of operation at the expected levels of output (after the set-up year) will be:

  (i) Direct labour — £4 million in the first year of production and sales.

(ii) Raw materials and bought-in parts — £3 million.

(iii) Management and Administrative costs — £800,000.

The company will depreciate £2 million of the cost of the manufacturing equipment for financial accounting purposes on a straight line basis over the 10 years of operation. £100,000 is expected to be recovered as scrap value when the project ends.

(iv) Marketing expenses will be £600,000 per annum.

(v) The working capital associated with the project will be £2.4 million, largely consisting of toasters that have been shipped to retail firms but have not yet been paid for. Working capital will build up during the set-up year and will run down during final year of sales and production.

The company pays tax at 30 per cent on its taxable profits with a lag of one year. The company will receive writing down allowances of 25 per cent per annum on a declining balance basis for its manufacturing equipment starting in the first year of sales and production. If the company goes ahead with the project it will finance the purchase of the property 50 per cent from the proceeds of selling certain land already owned by the company and 50 per cent by a £400,000 interest only mortgage. Property prices are expected to rise at 5 per cent per annum. Profits on disposal of property at the end of the project would be taxed as ordinary income, but the company expects that the building would not be sold but would continue to be used for other manufacturing operations. Manufacturing equipment would be partly purchased with a loan of £1.5 million at 11 per cent interest which would be repaid by 10 equal annual instalments of £254,700. Apart from these two items the debt level of the company would be unaffected by the new project.

Calculate the incremental after-tax cash flow of the toaster project.

References and Further Reading

Bierman, H. and Smidt, S. (1984) *The Capital Budgeting Decision*, 6th edn, MacMillan.

Miller, M.H. (1977) 'Debt and taxes', *Journal of Finance*, May, Vol. 32, No. 2, pp. 261–275.

Myers, S.C. (1974) 'Interactions of corporate financing and investment decisions — implications for capital budgeting', *Journal of Finance*, March, Vol. 29, No. 1, pp. 1–26.

3

Basic Discounting Techniques

Once the project cash flows have been identified, the next steps are:

(1) Specify the *required return* for the project. This number will be an annual percentage, similar to an interest rate.

(2) Use the cash flow and the required return in an *appraisal calculation* which leads to a decision to accept or reject the project.

This chapter deals with the second part of this process. We shall assume that a required rate of return, R, has already been set. Chapter 5 will explain how R can be chosen. It will be easier to discuss the selection of the rate when we have seen how it is used. There are two main types of appraisal calculation: *Net Present Value* and *Internal Rate of Return*. After we have discussed these we shall look at some popular but less correct alternatives. Finally, we shall look at the application of the recommended techniques in particular circumstances.

Net Present Value (NPV)

A required rate of return can be regarded as an exchange rate between cash that is received at different dates. A rate of 10 per cent ($= 0.10$) would mean that £1.00 in 1988 cash is equivalent in value to £1.00 (1.10) = £1.10 in 1989 cash. To get the 1990 equivalent, you multiply again by the annual growth factor of 1.10, giving £1.00 $\times$ $(1.10)^2$ = £1.21. In general, £1.00 now is equivalent to £1.00 $\times$ $(1 + R)^N$ in N years time, where R is the required rate. It can easily be seen that:

If £1.00 now is equivalent to £1.00 $(1 + R)^N$ in N years' time, then £1.00$/(1 + R)^N$ now is equivalent to £1.00 in N years' time.

The factors $(1 + R)^N$ [the future value of 1] and $1/(1 + R)^N$ [the present value of 1] are tabulated for a range of values in Tables 1 and 2 in the Appendix at the back of the book. Use of the other two tables is explained in the Appendix to this chapter (Interest Calculations). The phrase 'equivalent in value' means that the decision maker is indifferent between the two alternatives because either one can be exchanged for the other. It does not mean 'equivalent in purchasing power'. Normally an increase in purchasing power will be required when present cash is exchanged for future cash. The relationship between inflation and interest rates is discussed later.

The cash flow schedule for an investment project gives both cash amounts and the dates they are to be received. A Net Present Value calculation simply converts all the cash flows from a project (including the initial outlay) into their equivalents in current value and sums them. The total says how much the project is worth. A project with a positive net present value should be accepted. One with a negative NPV should be dropped. Our objective in making investment decisions is to increase shareholders' wealth. The NPV calculation tells us exactly what we want to know: how much the project would add to or subtract from the wealth represented by ownership of the business.

Think of a project as an abandoned suitcase containing money: if the amount of money is positive, you will pick up the suitcase and take the cash. If the suitcase contains 'negative cash' which would diminish your wealth, you will leave it alone. NPV simply tells you how much is in the suitcase. It gives the cash value, positive or negative, associated with the project. Mathematically, if I_0 is the immediate, initial cash outlay and C_i for $i = 1, \ldots, N$ is the cash inflow in the ith year, then:

$$\text{NPV} = -I_0 + \frac{C_1}{1 + R} + \frac{C_2}{(1 + R)^2} + \cdots + \frac{C_N}{(1 + R)^N}$$

$$= -I_0 + \sum_{i=1}^{N} \frac{C_i}{(1 + R)^i} \tag{3.1}$$

So, if:

$I_0 = 15,000$

$C_1 = 7,500$

$C_2 = 6,550$

$C_3 = 4,500$

and $R = 10\%$, then:

$$\text{NPV} = (15,000) + \frac{7,500}{1.10} + \frac{6,500}{(1.10)^2} + \frac{4,500}{(1.10)^3}$$

$$= 571$$

and the project should be accepted.

Internal Rate of Return (IRR)

Suppose that a bank or a government savings scheme offered a plan whereby a £100 deposit would, after five years, be worth £154: it would be natural to ask 'What rate of return does this scheme offer?' In this example, the solution is found by setting K as the unknown return and solving: 100 $(1 + K)^5 = 154$, from which $K = 0.09$ or 9 per cent.

Investment projects are just like deposits in the bank, but with a more complicated pattern of cash withdrawals. We can ask exactly the same question: 'What rate of return does this investment offer?' We find the answer by solving for the rate of return at which the present value of the cash inflows just matches the value of the cash outflows.

Solve for k:

$$I_0 = \frac{C_1}{1 + K} + \frac{C_2}{(1 + K)^2} + \cdots + \frac{C_N}{(1 + K)^N}$$

or:

$$O = -I_0 + \frac{C_1}{1 + K} + \frac{C_2}{(1 + K)^2} + \cdots + \frac{C_N}{(1 + K)^N}$$

This way of writing the equation makes it clear that the IRR is the required rate of return at which NPV is zero. Using the same numerical example that was used for NPV, we must solve:

$$O = -15,000 + \frac{7,500}{1 + K} + \frac{6,500}{(1 + K)^2} + \frac{4,500}{(1 + K)^3}$$

This equation can be solved by trial and error or, more simply, by a spreadsheet program that offers an IRR facility. Trial and error involves looking for a rate of return at which NPV is zero.

$$\text{Try 12\% NPV} = -15,000 + \frac{7,500}{1.12} + \frac{6,500}{(1.12)^2} + \frac{4,500}{(1.12)^3} = 81$$

$$\text{Try 13\% NPV} = -15,000 + \frac{7,500}{1.13} + \frac{6,500}{(1.13)^2} + \frac{4,500}{(1.13)^3} = -154$$

In this case the answer is clearly closer to 12% than 13%.

Using linear interpolation, we estimate the IRR as $12 \dfrac{81}{81 + 154}$

$$= 12.34\%$$

Using a spreadsheet gives the answer more accurately as 12.343%

Traditional Methods

There are two alternative approaches that have been sufficiently widely used
to warrant some comment:

Accounting Rate of Return

This calculation is based on incremental profit rather than incremental cash
flow. It is therefore dependent on the depreciation allowances. If the 15,000
initial investment in our example project was depreciated in three equal
instalments of 5,000 the incremental pre-tax profits would be 2,500; 1,500;
(500) for the three years respectively. We then calculate:

$$\text{Accounting Rate of Return} = \frac{\text{Average pre-tax incremental profit}}{\text{Average Investment}}$$

Since the investment has been depreciated in a straight line, the average

investment is $\dfrac{15,000}{2} = 7,500$

and Accounting Rate of Return $= \dfrac{1,167}{7,500} = 15.6\%$

Many businessmen's first notions of how to analyse an investment opportunity centre on some variant of accounting rate of return, so it is worth
pointing out what a poor measure it is. Suppose the project offered an
additional £500 of profit in year four instead of terminating at the end of
year three. This, of course, makes the project more attractive, but the new
accounting rate of return actually declines to 13.3 per cent. This is because
we are now averaging over four years rather than three. Average investment
is unchanged, but average incremental profit is now £1,000. The other
deficiencies are that the method uses profit rather than the more appropriate
measure of cash flow, and that it ignores the time value of money.

There are several variants of the accounting rate of return calculation.
The top line of the calculation can use either pre-tax or after-tax profits, and
the bottom line can use either average investment or initial investment. In
combination, these can give four different ways of calculating the
accounting rate of return for a project, and the highest and lowest measures
may well differ by a factor of three. It is not a useful method of project
appraisal.

Payback

Payback is the period of time before the cash inflows from a project match
the initial cash outlays. In our example project, the cash outlay is £15,000
and the inflow from the first two years is £14,000. The first £1,000 of the
£4,500 cash flow in year three is needed to recoup the initial investment. The
payback in this case is expressed as:

$$2 \frac{1000}{4500} = 2.22 \text{ years}$$

Some companies set a payback requirement for their projects. Two or three
years is often set as the standard. It should be clear from the earlier
arguments that this is a thoroughly unsatisfactory way of making decisions.
One weakness is that payback takes no account of the time value of money.
A more serious one is that payback is not remotely connected to the net
benefit which a product brings. Consider projects x and y with cash flow as
follows:

			cash flow (£)		
Project	Initial Outlay	Year 1	Year 2	Year 3	Years 4 to 20
x	60,000	20,001	20,001	20,001	0
y	60,000	19,999	19,999	19,999	19,999

Project x has a payback slightly less than three years and project y has a
payback that is slightly more. Project x seems better. But this ignores cash
flow beyond the payback period. For project x this is negligible. For project
y there is a substantial cash flow for another 17 years. Since the net benefit
from any project comes from cash flow after payback, it is entirely illogical
to ignore these cash flows in the appraisal decision.

  Payback is, therefore, a very poor way of making investment decisions.
It may be worth calculating, though, for an entirely different reason. Some
projects yield their benefits more quickly than others, and the decision
maker may well be interested in a numerical measure of how fast the cash
comes back. Future financing decisions, for example, must take account of
cash generated by the firm's investment projects, and a summary measure
can be useful. There are two available alternatives:

(1) Discounted payback Ordinary payback takes no account of the time
value of money. Discounted payback does. For the Nth year, the discounted
cash flow is:

$$\frac{C_N}{(1 + R)^N}$$

These discounted cash flows are then used to calculate payback in the usual way. For our example project, where $R = 10$ per cent, we have:

	Now	year 1	year 2	year 3
Cash flow (£)	(15,000)	7,500	6,500	4,500
Discounted cash flow (£)	(15,000)	6,818	5,372	3,381
Cumulative discounted cash flow (£)	(15,000)	(8,182)	(2,810)	571

Notice that cumulative discounted cash flow over the whole life of the project is just the NPV. From this, it can be seen that the project requires 2,810 out of the discounted cash flow for year three to break even, giving a discounted payback of:

$$2\,\frac{2,810}{3,381} \; = \; 2.83 \text{ years}$$

(2) Duration   This measures the average period of time before the benefits of the project (measured as discounted cash flow) are received. The total benefits to be received are:

$$\sum_{i=1}^{N} \frac{C_i}{(1 + R)^i} \; = \; NPV + I_0$$

The fraction of total benefits that are received (for example) in the second year is:

$$\frac{\left[\dfrac{C_2}{(1 + R)^2}\right]}{NPV + I_0}$$

This is the weight given to two years in the calculation of duration. Notice that the sum of the weights must equal one. To calculate duration, each year in the project's life $(1, 2, \ldots, N)$ is multiplied by the appropriate weight and the resulting numbers are added together.

$$\text{Duration} \; = \; \sum_{i=1}^{N} \frac{\left[\dfrac{C_i}{(1 + R)^i}\right] \cdot i}{NPV + I_0}$$

Calculations in Table 3.1 show that duration for our example is 1.78 years. Duration is the best one-number answer to the question 'How long do we wait to get the benefits from this project?'

Table 3.1

Year	Discounted Cash Flow (DCF)	Weight = $\dfrac{DCF}{NPV + I_0}$	Year × Weight
1	6,818	0.438	0.438
2	5,372	0.345	0.690
3	3,381	0.217	0.651
Total	15,571	1.000	1.779
	$(NPV + I_0)$		(Duration)

Combining the Measures

The ready availability of spreadsheet programs with graphic facilities makes it easy to present these project analysis measures in the form of a diagram which shows the cumulative discounted cash flow at a range of different discount rates above and below the required rate. The Internal Rate of Return is the discount rate at which the cumulative discounted cash flow is zero. Using several different discount rates can be helpful because, as we shall see later, there can be doubt about what the correct required rate is.

For this example, the company's required rate of return is taken to be 15 per cent and the project cash flows are:

	Now	Years 1–12
Cash Flow	(50,000)	10,000

Figure 3.1 shows the cumulative discounted cash flows at the required return (15 per cent) and at rates 3 per cent above and below this figure. Three per cent is a generous allowance for uncertainty surrounding the required rate.

Discounted payback can be read off the diagram directly, at the point where cumulative discounted cash flow cuts the horizontal axis. IRR can also be estimated, as it is the discount rate at which cumulative discounted cash flow is zero at the end of the project's life. The diagram also gives a graphic depiction of the cash flow consequences of the project and an estimate of the effect of cutting short the project's life (or of extending it). A spreadsheet program can easily be used to create this sort of graphic display for any project once the cash flow is specified.

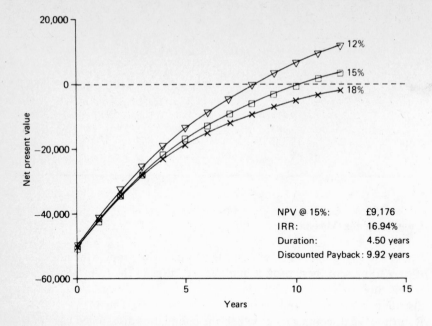

Figure 3.1 Cumulative Discounted Cash Flow

Difficulties with DCF Techniques

In many cases, either NPV or IRR are both perfectly good techniques for project appraisal and it is a matter of personal preference which of the two the decision maker uses. There are, however, several situations where one or both of the methods can create difficulties. The four situations, which we shall consider in turn, are:

(1) Interdependent projects
(2) Unconventional cash flow patterns
(3) Non-constant required rate of return
(4) Capital rationing

(1) Interdependent Projects

Independent projects are ones which stand alone, and the decision to accept or reject one project can be made quite separately from the decisions on other projects. *Interdependent* projects are ones which are linked in one of two ways:

(a) *Mutually exclusive projects* If you accept *A*, then you cannot also accept *B*. This commonly occurs when two or more projects would both use the same resource — vacant space in the corner of the factory, for example.

(b) *Pre-requisite projects* You can only accept project *D* if you also accept project *C*. An example of this would arise when a company plans a new facility for chemical manufacture. This is often a multi-stage project, with a range of intermediate products being produced within the complex which are then combined in various chemical processes to yield the end product. A decision to install equipment and to manufacture a product for outside sale can only be taken if it is also decided to install the necessary production facilities and to manufacture the precursor products. There may be several precursors for one final product. The decision to manufacture one precursor may make it possible to produce several extra final products.

Mutually Exclusive Projects

Suppose that projects *A* and *B* are mutually exclusive. There is no problem in deciding what to do unless both of the projects, appraised individually, are acceptable. In this case we are faced with the problem of *ranking* projects:

Let project *A* be the example project we have already used in this chapter, and project *B* a mutually exclusive alternative. The cash flows for both *A* and *B* are shown below:

		Cash Flow (£)		
Project	*Now*	*Year 1*	*Year 2*	*Year 3*
A	(15,000)	7,500	6,500	4,500
B	(15,000)	10,000	6,900	1,000

NPV and IRR for these two projects are:

Project	*NPV at 10%*	*IRR*
A	571	12.34%
B	544	12.72%

The two decision criteria give different rankings. *A* has a higher NPV than *B*, but *B* has a higher IRR than *A*. In these circumstances, the *NPV ranking should be preferred*, and project *A* accepted. Recall that NPV is the best measure of our decision-making objective. It tells us how much money we shall make, and an opportunity to make £571 is better than an opportunity to make £544.

Why has the conflict of rankings occurred, and what is wrong with the IRR approach? The weakness of IRR is that it ignores the scale of the project, both in terms of the amount of the initial investment and the period for which it will last. An opportunity to invest at 100 per cent per annum return sounds very good. But in rating this project *vis-à-vis* alternatives it is surely relevant to know that only £100 can be invested at that rate, or that the project will only last for a few months. IRR ignores these scale factors, while NPV takes them into account.

In this example, we have preferred project *A* to project *B*. Notice that this decision is conditional on the required rate of return being 10 per cent. We might reach a different conclusion with a different required rate. If the required rate was 12.50 per cent, for example, project *A* would be unacceptable because it only offers an IRR of 12.34 per cent. Project *B* remains acceptable and would therefore be chosen. How the attractiveness of the two projects varies with the required rate is shown in Figure 3.2. This plots NPV for the two projects against the required return. The plotted lines for the two projects cross. Because *A* is a longer-lasting project (it has a duration of 1.78 years compared to 1.46 years for project *B*), its NPV is more sensitive to discount rate charges. There is nothing mysterious about the two lines having different slopes, or about them intersecting. When this occurs there

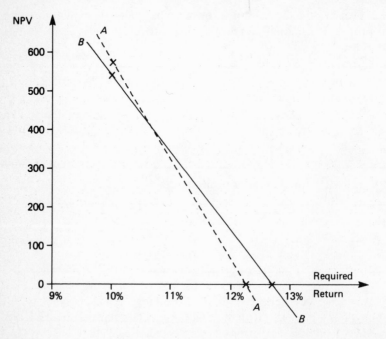

Figure 3.2

Table 3.2

Project	Cash Flows (£)			
	Now	Year 1	Year 2	Year 3
A	(15,000)	7,500	6,500	4,500
B	(15,000)	10,000	6,900	1,100
A–B	0	(2,500)	(400)	3,500

is always the possibility of a conflict between the NPV ranking and the IRR ranking.

If the decision maker really wants to use the IRR approach, it is still possible to show that A is the better choice. Consider the *incremental project* (A–B). The cash flows are calculated as shown in Table 3.2. The incremental project must have an NPV of 27, because NPVs are additive and:

$$\text{NPV}_{A-B} = \text{NPV}_A - \text{NPV}_B = 571 - 544 = 27$$

Its IRR is 10.67 per cent and this means that project (A–B) is acceptable in its own right. If you accept project B and also accept project (A–B), this means that you are in practice accepting project A. It seems simpler to get the right answer first time using the NPV approach.

Prerequisite Projects

Consider a company designing a chemical plant. It can produce various precursor chemicals and could sell these to other companies for further processing. Alternatively, it could 'buy' part of the output of the precursors itself and make a final product. The NPVs of the precursor projects and the final products projects are given in Table 3.3. The NPVs for the precursors assume all output is sold outside the company. The NPVs for the final products assume that the inputs are bought at market prices. The first thing to notice is that the product set can be partitioned. R and M have links with each other but no links with the rest of the group. This set of two can be treated separately. These are effectively two alternatives, M on its own, or M and R together. The aggregate NPV of each alternative can be calculated, and the highest NPV chosen.

Projects	Aggregate NPV
M	+£2m
M and R	+£1m

M should be selected, but not R.

Table 3.3

Precursor products	NPV (£m)	Final products	NPV (£m)	Precursors
J	−10	P	+10	J, K
K	−2	Q	+4	L, J
L	+4	R	−1	M
M	+2			

For the remaining projects it is necessary first to list the available alternatives. *L, P* and *Q* show positive NPVs on their own. We list all combinations of these three projects, list the precursors needed for each combination, and work out the aggregate NPV in each case for the profitable products and their precursors together (see Table 3.4). The combination of projects giving the highest aggregate NPV is then selected. In this example, it is *(P, Q, J, K, L)* plus *M*, selected already.

Table 3.4

Combination of profitable projects	Precursors	Aggregate NPV (£m)
L	—	4
P	J, K	−2
Q	J, L	−2
L, P	J, K	+2
L, Q	J	−2
P, Q	J, K, L	+6
P, Q, L	J, K	+6

More complex interrelationships between projects are sometimes best approached by Decision Tree Analysis. This technique is not covered here but is explained by Magee (1964).

(2) Unconventional Cash Flow Patterns

Conventional cash flows involve cash outflows for the first *m* years of an *n* year project (*m < n*) and cash inflows for all subsequent years.

Reverse cash flows consist of cash inflows for the first *m* years followed by cash outflows for the remaining *n–m* years. *Complex* cash flows involve more than one change of sign in the cash flows and cover all cases which follow neither the conventional pattern nor the reverse pattern. An example would be an open-cast mining project where there is an initial cash outflow to buy equipment and clear the overburden, years of cash inflow while coal is extracted, and finally a cash outflow to cover the cost of restoring and landscaping the site.

Reverse Cash Flows

We have already drawn the analogy between the cash flows from a conventional project and making a bank deposit. For a reverse cash flow project the analogy is with taking out a bank loan. The cash inflow comes first, followed by cash outflows. NPV calculations for a reverse cash flow project have exactly the same interpretation as those for a conventional project. Not so for IRR. Because a reverse cash flow project is like a loan, a *lower* rate of return makes the project more attractive. You accept a reverse cash flow project if the IRR is *less* than the required rate of return. The logic of this is made clear by a plot of NPV against discounted rate for this type of project as illustrated in Figure 3.3. The cash flows used in this example are:

Year	Now	1	2	3	4
Cash Flow	+2,000	(600)	(600)	(600)	(600)

Unlike a conventional project, the line is upward sloping and the positive NPV are to be found at discount rates higher than the IRR.

Unconventional Cash Flows

Consider a project with the following cash flows:

Year	Now	1	2	3
Cash Flow	(10,000)	34,500	(39,650)	15,180

It turns out that for this project there are three solutions to the IRR equation: 10 per cent, 15 per cent and 20 per cent. There is a ready explanation for this number of solutions. If we let $S = 1/1 + K$, then the IRR equation can be rewritten for a three year project as:

$$0 = -I_o + C_1 S + C_2 S^2 + C_3 S^2$$

This is a cubic equation and can be expected to have three solutions. A plot

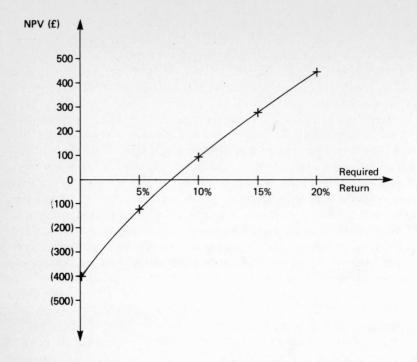

Figure 3.3

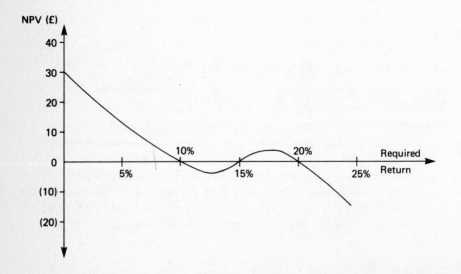

Figure 3.4

of NPV against the discount rate is shown in Figure 3.4. A two-year project would give a quadratic equation and two solutions. In general, an n-year project would have n different internal rates of return.

In most cases, though, multiple internal rates of return will not occur. Mathematically, solutions to polynomial equations can be real or can involve imaginary numbers. Imaginary numbers (involving the square root of -1) are of no interest in the present context. According to the theorem known as the Descartes Rule of Signs, the number of real solutions is equal to the number of changes of sign in the sequence of coefficients. The coefficients in our context are the cash flows. A conventional project, or a reverse cash flow project, will therefore only have one IRR. The example at the beginning of this section had a cash flow pattern $- + - +$. There are three changes of sign in this sequence so there are three real solutions.

Unconventional cash flow patterns are not uncommon. A property company developing a site may erect one building and sell it, then erect another and sell that, and so on. This will produce the kind of cash flow that can give multiple returns.

When multiple IRRs create a problem, use NPV. The NPV method works perfectly well for any pattern of cash flow, and will lead to the right decision without complication. For the example used above, the project is acceptable if the required rate of return is below 10 per cent or between 15 per cent and 20 per cent. It is not acceptable if the required return is between 10 per cent and 15 per cent or is over 20 per cent.

(3) Non-Constant Required Rate of Return

The required rate of return will be linked to market interest rates. It will be somewhat higher than interest rates. This reflects the fact that interest rates usually relate to risk-free transactions, but business projects are risky. Extra risk requires extra reward.

The link is therefore a loose one, but when interest rates rise, required rates of return will normally rise too. One problem is that interest rates vary according to the length of the loan. In 1980 the one-year interest rate was up around 17 per cent while the 10-year rate was about 14 per cent. In 1975, the one-year rate was 11 per cent while the 10-year rate was about 14 per cent. Using the NPV technique it is possible to set R_i as the required rate of return for cash flow arriving i years into the future. It is then possible to calculate an NPV using different required returns for the different years in which cash flow will be received:

$$\text{NPV} = -I_0 + \sum_{i=1}^{N} \frac{C_i}{(1 + R_i)^i}$$

The IRR technique cannot be used if the required rate of return is non-constant. Although interest rates for different years are usually sufficiently close for a single required rate to be used, it is worth noting that the NPV method can be adapted to allow for varying rates.

(4)   Capital Rationing

Often a business will find itself with a fixed limited amount of money available for investment and more than enough good projects on which to spend it. How should projects be selected in this case? The capital rationing problem is one with a voluminous literature, and this is a sign that it has not been fully cracked. The existence of capital rationing violates one of the major assumptions of project appraisal theory, namely, that there are perfectly competitive financial markets from which money can be obtained whenever commercially justified and in which surplus funds can always be placed. It is by the standards of this market that cash flows can be valued. Without such a standard it is only possible to give limited, conditional and rule-of-thumb answers to the capital rationing problem.

Capital rationing is likely to arise in two cases:

(1) Smaller companies and new, unproven ventures often have limited access to financial markets, particularly equity markets. Every approach to these markets requires a major exercise in preparing figures and forecasts and presenting them to the financial community. In these cases capital availability is fixed in the short term, but the period of capital rationing is unlikely to last more than one or two years.

(2) Divisions of large companies are often allocated investment budgets. If these are determined arbitrarily (or by intra-organisational politics) rather than a rational allocation of resources, the divisions may find that they face a capital rationing problem. In this case the problem may be a long-term one.

Short-Term Rationing

The assumption here is that the company is cut off from access to the financial markets for a short period, say one year. It has available now a list of all the investment projects it might undertake during the rationing period and these projects cannot be 'frozen'. If they are not accepted at this time it will not be possible to accept them later. The company has a fixed amount of money available for investment now, and it knows the required

rate of return on its projects which is justified by the current state of the
financial markets, even though it has no access to these markets.

Under these circumstances it is appropriate to rank projects according to
their *Profitability Index* (PI). This is defined for a conventional project as:

$$PI = \frac{\text{Present Value of Cash Inflows}}{\text{Initial Cash Outlay}} = \frac{\sum_{i=1}^{N} \frac{C_i}{(1 + R)^i}}{I_0}$$

Note that the present value of cash inflows is simply the NPV plus the initial
cash outlay, so we can also write:

$$PI = \frac{I_0 + NPV}{I_0} = 1 + \frac{NPV}{I_0}$$

It is clear from the last equation that projects with a positive NPV will have
a PI greater than one.

Suppose that we have an investment budget of £500,000 and five projects
are available (as shown in Table 3.5). Ranking in order of PI puts *D* first
and then *E* and *B*. This uses up all the budget. Naturally, ranking by PI
gives a different selection than if we had ranked by NPV or IRR. The use
of PI in this type of problem is entirely consistent with having NPV as our
basic objective. PI measures the gain in NPV per unit of the scarce resource,
investment funds. *Selecting by PI ensures that we get the largest aggregate
NPV from the available projects.* Our example illustrates this. Ranking by
PI gives a total NPV of £175,000. Ranking by NPV will spend all the budget
on project *A*. Ranking by IRR will select projects *C*, *D* and *E*. In both cases
the total NPV is only £125,000. Profitability Index seems a very natural
measure of a project's attractiveness. It is often misused. Its correct use is
strictly reserved for capital rationing situations. There are two possible
complications in the use of the PI technique.

Table 3.5

Project	Initial Outlay (£)	NPV (£)	IRR	PI
A	50,000	125,000	28%	1.25
B	250,000	75,000	22%	1.30
C	150,000	25,000	40%	1.17
D	100,000	50,000	30%	1.50
E	150,000	50,000	30%	1.33

Table 3.6

Project	Initial outlay (£)	NPV (£)	PI
A	100,000	50,000	1.50
B	300,000	90,000	1.30
C	200,000	50,000	1.25
D	200,000	50,000	1.25
E	250,000	50,000	1.20

(1) Lumpiness   If you follow the PI ranking you may find that a significant part of your investment budget remains unspent. But you cannot accept the next project on the list because it is a large one and you would then have overspent. The objective in using the PI rule is to maximise the total Net Present Value of accepted projects. It may be necessary to break the rule slightly if the alternative is to leave a lot of the budget unallocated. Take, for example, an investment budget of £500,000 and look at Table 3.6. It is better to accept *A*, *C* and *D* rather than *A* and *B*. The answer is found by ignoring *B*, which is the lowest acceptable project on a PI basis, and trying projects further down the list to see if they can give a higher aggregate NPV.

(2) Postponability   The PI approach assumes that projects cannot be postponed. In practice some have a much longer 'shelf-life' than others. A cost reduction project involving equipment replacement will still be there next year if it is not taken up now; an opportunity to acquire another company will not. This situation can be handled by calculating a 'Cost of Delay Index' where:

$$\text{CDI} = \frac{\text{NPV if immediately accepted} - \text{NPV if delayed to end of capital rationing}}{\text{Initial Cash Outlay}}$$

and using CDI in the same way as PI.

Long-Term Rationing

In this case we suppose that the company or division is given an arbitrary (or at least exogenously determined) sum each year for investment purposes. This situation is expected to continue indefinitely.

It is, of course, silly to allocate investment funds without regard to the availability of profitable projects. In this section we pose a foolish question and there can be no surprise if we fail to come up with a sensible answer. The financial markets are not closed on a long-term basis to any business with good prospects, so that long-term capital rationing can only arise from the company's own internal policies. Shareholders' wealth (constrained by arbitrary rationing of investment funds) is bound to be less than if the constraints were lifted. The only real solution is to change company policies so that fund availability is adjusted to match the availability of good projects, rather than fitting the chosen projects within a straitjacket of available funds.

There are two approaches which can be of some limited help in situations of long-term capital rationing:

(1) An IRR cut-off   With investment funds fixed, the problem is really one of how to invest this money to achieve the highest return. If you could find a rate of return higher than the normal rate required, such that you could just use up your investment allocation in each time period on projects offering an IRR at this level or above, then the problem would be solved. It is, of course, unlikely that the same required IRR would exactly match the supply and demand for funds in each time period, but this approach might be the best rule-of-thumb under the circumstances. Note that PI would not work here. PI can lead to the acceptance of long-lived projects with very modest IRR. With short-term rationing this does not matter: next period, you will be able to get all the funds you need. With long-term rationing, long-lived projects which look good on a PI basis may tie up funds and choke off good projects in later years.

(2) Linear programming   The most sophisticated way to fit projects within fixed investment budgets is linear programming. Linear programming (LP) is a mathematical optimisation technique well suited to the use of computers.

Formulating any problem in order that it can be solved using LP requires us to set an objective function which we wish to maximise, plus a set of constraints. The objective function for the capital rationing problem is clear enough: we want to maximise the aggregate Net Present Value of all the projects that we accept. This NPV is expressed in current money, although some of the projects will be launched several years in the future. The constraints are that the company must keep within its cash flow limits. Mathematically, there is a separate constraint for each year. The amount invested in any year cannot exceed the total of:

(1) the funds carried over from the previous year;

(2) the unused debt capacity of the firm; and

(3) the cash generated by existing projects and activities during the year.

With this information, the computer will give impressive results. The solution will tell the company which projects to launch in each year. It will do the job neatly, 'jig-sawing' the projects together so that they fit within the cash constraints. It may pick a project of no obvious outstanding merit in one year because the program calculates that it will bring cash back at just the right time to enable another highly profitable project to be launched at a later date.

The real difficulty with this approach is not mathematical: it is simply that the information required as input is far more than most businesses have available. The program has to know the cash flows from all the possible investment projects that might be accepted during the planning period. A project may have different cash flows depending on the date it is initiated, and the computer must have these numbers too. An additional set of constraints specifies that no project can be initiated more than once.

The real world of business is rarely like this. Firms have to respond flexibly to an environment in which opportunities are continually opening up or terminating. They simply do not know what investment projects will be available five years into the future, and therefore have to rely on the simpler capital rationing techniques described earlier.

There is one exception to this. Natural resource companies involved in oil, gold mining or timber can take a much longer view. An oil company may have proven oil reserves today that it may not develop for years. Linear programming may well be useful in deciding in which order to develop the company's reserves, knowing the cost of putting each field into production and its potential yield. Further information on the technique can be found in Weingartner (1963 and 1977).

Inflation

One of the main causes of errors in capital investment analysis is failure to incorporate inflation correctly. The danger comes from a combination of two practices each of which, considered on its own, seems very reasonable.

(1) Future costs and revenues are estimated assuming a continuation of current price levels. Governments often promise (or threaten) a reduction in inflation to negligible levels, and businesses are reluctant to undertake projects where they are relying on inflation to provide the profit.

(2) The required rate of return is set at a level based on current market interest rates. In simple terms, the business decides that its projects must cover the cost of borrowing from the bank, with something extra on top to allow for business risk.

To show that these two policies are inconsistent, consider the break-down of market interest rates. They consist of two parts, expected inflation and a real return. If:

N = market interest rate
I = expected inflation
and R = real return
then $1 + N = (+ R)(1 = I)$

This formula may seem surprising. The relationship is often assumed to be;

$N = R + I$

When N, R and I are all small, this is a close approximation, but it is easy to demonstrate that it is not generally correct. Suppose $N = 21$ per cent and $I = 10$ per cent. Suppose for simplicity that the basket of goods that makes up the inflation index contains only potatoes, and that potatoes currently cost 10p per lb. Now consider the changes between this year and next year:

	This year	Comment	Next year
Cash	£1.00	Nominal interest 21%	£1.21
Price level	10p/lb	Inflation 10%	11p/lb
Purchasing power	10 lbs	Real return 10%	11 lbs

This shows that an individual who has a purchasing power of 10 lbs of potatoes this year will, if he saves rather than spends, be able to buy 11 lbs next year. This is a 10 per cent real return. So if $N = 21$ per cent and $I = 10$ per cent, $R = 10$ per cent. This confirms the accuracy of the formula:

$1 + N = (1 + R)(1 + I)$

since $1.21 = (1.10)(1.10)$

The real rate of return is determined by basic forces in the economy, principally by the opportunities for productive investment and willingness of individuals to postpone consumption. It has averaged about 2–3 per cent in recent decades. The inflation component of interest rates is more volatile and has no natural level. Recent financial history has been characterised by steep unanticipated rises and falls in the inflation level, which is fundamentally determined by government monetary policy. Since the 1960s inflation has been the larger of the two components of market interest rates.

For consistency, inflation must either be included in *both* the cash flows and the required rate of return, or in neither. Suppose that $C_1, C_2, \ldots, C_N$ are the projected cash flows at *present* price levels. K is the required rate of return, which is greater than market interest rates by a factor F to allow for business risk. The form of the relationship is as follows:

$(1 + K) = (1 + N)(1 + F) = (1 + R)(1 + I)(1 + F)$

Suppose, further, that inflation would affect all the elements of cash flow equally, so that the nominal cash flows from the project are:

$$C_1(1 + I), C_2(1 + I)^2, \ldots, C_N(1 + I)^N$$

If inflation is consistently included, then the calculation of NPV is:

$$\text{NPV} = -I_0 + \frac{C_1(1 + I)}{1 + K} + \frac{C_2(1 + I)^2}{(1 + K)^2} + \cdots + \frac{C_N(1 + I)^N}{(1 + K)^N}$$

If inflation is consistently taken out, then required discount factor becomes $(1 + R)(1 + F) = 1 + K/1 + I$ instead of $1 + K$. In this case:

$$\text{NPV} = -I_0 + \frac{C_1}{(1 + R)(1 + F)} + \frac{C_2}{(1 + R)^2(1 + F)^2} + \cdots$$

$$+ \frac{C_N}{(1 + R)^N(1 + F)^N}$$

These two methods of calculating NPV give exactly the same result since, choosing one term for illustration —

$$\frac{C_1(1 + I)}{1 + K} = \frac{C_1(1 + I)}{(1 + R)(1 + I)(1 + F)} = \frac{C_1}{(1 + R)(1 + F)}$$

The choice between the two methods is governed by convenience. Usually inflation will have a different impact on different parts of the project. Wage costs are likely to grow faster than inflation. Prices of many consumer durables tend to rise more slowly. It is generally recommended, therefore, that the impact of inflation be separately forecast for the individual components of cash flow and that they be aggregated into cash flows that incorporate expected inflation.

For some very long-lived projects (the construction of reservoirs for water supply is an example), the decision makers may be reluctant to forecast inflation far into the future. Present price levels for the cash flows can be used, as long as the required rate of return used in the calculation is the required *real* rate of return.

Estimating Future Inflation

Most of the world has to rely on econometric models to forecast inflation. In the UK we have the benefit of being able to observe market expectations directly. Market expectations are likely to take into account a broader range of factors and to be more sensitive to novel developments in the economic environment. The UK government issues index-linked securities. With slight simplification, it can be said that these are like ordinary fixed interest, government guaranteed stock except that all interest payments and the final repayment of principal are increased in the same proportion as the rise in the Retail Price Index since the stock was issued. The stated or 'coupon' rate of return offered when the stock is issued is therefore a real rate of return;

the investor will get protection against inflation on top. The real rate of return can be calculated from the market price at any time during the life of the bond, and this rate is quoted in the financial press every day.

Using 1 October 1987 as the base date, let us assume we wish to calculate the expected level of inflation over the next nine years approximately:

Yield on 2% Index Linked Stock maturing 1996 $= 4.09\% = R$

Yield on 10% Conventional Gilt-Edged Stock maturing 1996 $=$

$10.37\% = N$

Hence, $1 + I = \dfrac{1 + N}{1 + R} = \dfrac{1.1037}{1.0409} = 1.0603$

and $I \simeq 6\%$

There are minor uncertainties surrounding this calculation. Indexation of index-linked securities is not perfect. Because of the interest component in the cash flows, the match between the two stocks is not perfect and the inflation calculation is weighted towards the values expected in the earlier part of the nine-year period. Also, the RPI figures are based on a basket of consumer goods, and industrial prices might move slightly differently.

In relation to the other uncertainties in capital investment appraisal, these are minor problems. The rate of inflation in the year prior to October 1987 was 3.8 per cent. The calculation therefore tells us that inflation was expected to rise significantly, and that this expectation was built into current interest rates. Net Present Value calculations should be adjusted accordingly.

Appendix: Using Interest Rate Tables

There are four interest rate tables in the Appendix at the back of this book. They are:

Table 1   Present value of 1
Table 2   Future value of 1
Table 3   Present value of an annuity of 1
Table 4   Terminal value of an annuity of 1.

Table 1 lists values of $1/(1 + r)^n$ for various combinations of r and n. It gives, therefore, the present value of £1 due to be received in n years at an interest rate of r. For all positive values of r and n the numbers *in this table are less than unity.*

Example 1   What is the present value of £5,500 to be received in seven years' time if the interest rate is 12 per cent? Looking up the table for $r = 12$ per cent and $n = 7$, we find a present value factor of 0.4523. Each pound to be received has a present value slightly greater than 45p, and the present value of £5,500 is:

$$5,500 \times 0.4523 = £2,488$$

Table 2 gives the value that would be reached at the end of n years if an amount of 1 were invested now and received compound interest at the rate of r per cent over the intervening period. The numbers in the table therefore give $(1 + r)^n$ for combinations of r and n. *All the values in the table will be greater than 1.*

Example 2   £3,200 is deposited in a bank. If it receives 9 per cent interest compounded annually, what will the value of the deposit be at the end of 10 years? Looking up Table 2 for $r = 9$ per cent and $n = 10$ gives 2.3674. Each £1 invested will therefore have grown to almost £2.37. The value of the whole deposit will be:

$$3,200 \times 2.3674 = £7,575.7$$

Table 3 is the first of the annuity tables. An annuity is an equal annual payment that is made or received each year. Table 3 gives the present value of a sequence of annual payments of £1. The first payment is assumed to be one year into the future and the last is n years into the future, so there are n payments in the annuity altogether. The formula for the value of this annuity is:

$$\frac{1}{1 + r} + \frac{1}{(1 + r)^2} + \frac{1}{(1 + r)^3} + \cdots + \frac{1}{(1 + r)^n}$$

This is the sum of a geometric series and can also be written as:

$$\frac{1}{r}\left[1 - \frac{1}{(1 + r)^n}\right]$$

For $n = 1$, the values in Table 3 are less than 1. For $n > 1$ the values are above unity but somewhat less than n.

Example 3   A national lottery offers a first prize of £1,000,000. This will be paid to the lucky winner in 20 annual instalments of £50,000, with the first payment in one year. At an interest rate of 10 per cent, what is the value of the prize in present value terms? The entry in Table 3 for $n = 20$ and $r = 10$ per cent is 8.5136, so the value of the prize is:

$$50,000 \times 8.5136 = £425,680$$

An annuity that starts in one year is called, surprisingly, an immediate annuity. A series of annual payments that starts now is called an annuity due. The tables can be used directly for an immediate annuity. For an annuity due it is easiest to use the tables to value all the payments except the first one and simply add on the initial payment which, of course, does not need to be discounted. Notice that when you take away the first payment, an n-year annuity is turned into an $n - 1$-year annuity.

Example 4   Suppose that the first of the 20 annual payments of £50,000 to the lottery winner was made immediately after the draw. What would the present value of the prize be then? Again we assume a 10 per cent interest rate. Taking out the first payment we have a 19-year immediate annuity at 10 per cent. From Table 3 the valuation factor is 8.3649. So the value of the annuity is:

50,000 × 8.3649 = £418,245

adding back the first payment of £50,000 shows the total value of the prize to be £468,245.

Finally, **Table 4** shows the terminal value of the annuity. This is the total value after $n - 1$ years of a series of n equal annual payments which attract interest at an annual compound rate of r per cent. The assumption here is that the first payment is made now (hence the nth payment comes after $n - 1$ years), and the expression evaluated in the table is:

$$1 + (1 + r) + (1 + r)^2 + \ldots + (1 + r)^{n-1}$$

which simplifies to:

$$\frac{(1 + r)^n - 1}{r}$$

For $n = 1$ the values in the table are unity for all values of r. For $n > 1$, the values in the table are always greater than n.

Example 5   An investor saves £3,000 each year on his birthday starting with his 41st birthday. He deposits the money in a bank which offers 11 per cent interest compounded annually. What will be the value of his account when he retires on his 60th birthday, just after making his last annual deposit? In this case there are 20 annual payments, and the value in Table 4 for $n = 20$ and $r = 11$ per cent is 64.2028. The final value in his account is therefore:

3,000 × 64.2028 = £192,608

The numbers in the interest rate tables can be replicated very quickly on a calculator if the appropriate formula is at hand. It is often hard to remember the formula and quicker to look the number up in the tables. Spreadsheet packages for personal computers also often have interest and annuity factors built in.

Study Questions

1. Calculate the NPV, the IRR, the payback, the discounted payback and the profitability index for a project with the following incremental after-tax cash flows. The required rate of return is 15 per cent.

Initial Outlay	£25,000
Cash flow after 1 year	£ 9,572
Cash flow after 2 years	£ 8,702
Cash flow after 3 years	£ 7,831
Cash flow after 4 years	£ 6,961
Cash flow after 5 years	£ 5,221

2. Calculate the NPV and IRR for a project with the following incremental after-tax cash flows. The required rate of return is 8 per cent.

Initial Outlay	£133,000
Cash Flow after 1 year	£103,000
Cash Flow after 2 years	£ 84,000
Cash Flow after 3 years	£ 39,000
Cash Flow after 4 years	£ 7,000
Cash Flow after 5 years	£(88,000)

3. A large energy company is considering three possible investments. The company has a required return of 15 per cent, and pays no corporation tax.

   (a) Develop the 'Quaich' oilfield in the North Sea using tankers to collect the oil from a buoy and to bring it ashore. The features of this project are:

      (i) Initial investment as of 31.13.84 — £550m, of which £50m has very recently been spent on exploration and the remainder is destined for the installation of the buoy and the purchase of tankers.

      (ii) A net annual cash flow of £90m per year from 1985 to 1999. At the end of 1999, when the field will run dry, the scrap value of the buoy and tankers will be £125m.

   (b) Develop the 'Quaich' oilfield using a pipeline to bring the oil ashore. This requires a larger capital investment but has low running costs and will get the oil out quickly. The details are:

      (i) Initial investment as of 31.12.82 is £1,050m. As with project A, £50m has already been spent on exploration and the remainder is for installing the pipeline and associated equipment.

(ii) A net annual cash flow of £250m per annum from 1985 to 1991 inclusive. There is no scrap value for the pipeline.

(c) Develop an opencast coal field in the US, in which no investment has been made so far. The details are:

(i) An investment of £50m by 31.12.84.
(ii) A cash flow of £50m in each year from 1985 to 1992.
(iii) The pit must be filled in and the landscape restored in 1993, at a total cost of £350m.

The energy company is not limited to accepting only one project, but projects (*a*) and (*b*) are mutually exclusive. If neither (*a*) nor (*b*) is accepted, the costs of exploration must be written off completely. Calculate:

(1) the NPV for each investment
(2) the IRR for each investment
(3) the payback for each investment

Which project(s) do you recommend for acceptance?

4. The following information is given for six projects which are being considered by a company. They all have conventional cash flow patterns.

Project	Initial outlay	NPV at 20%	NPV at 12%	IRR
A	45,000	5,500	7,550	28%
B	70,000	5,000	8,000	24%
C	30,000	(2,500)	3,000	18%
D	85,000	8,000	12,500	22%
E	55,000	7,000	11,000	26%
F	15,000	(10,000)	(4,000)	8%

Which projects should be accepted if:

(a) All projects are independent, and the required rate of return is 20 per cent.
(b) A and B are mutually exclusive; D and E are mutually exclusive; the required rate of return is 12 per cent.
(c) Project C is a prerequisite for project B; project F is a prerequisite for project E; the required rate of return is 20 per cent.
(d) There is a temporary limit on funds available during the current year of £200,000. None of the projects will be available after the end of the current year. The required rate of return is 20 per cent.
(e) There is a temporary limit of funds available during the current year of £175,000. None of the projects will be available beyond the end of the current year. The required rate of return is 12 per cent.

5. An index-linked gilt that will be redeemed in eight years offers a yield to redemption of 3.11 per cent. A conventional gilt with the same maturity date offers a redemption yield of 9.11 per cent. Estimate the likely level of inflation over the eight-year period.

6. A manufacturing company is considering an investment in a new automated central warehouse. The new system would cost £60,000 to install and is expected to last for 10 years. There will be no net scrap value. The company would simultaneously close down two other, smaller warehouses and sell off the property. These warehouses are held on a lease which has 10 years to run. The remaining portion of the lease can be sold for £370,000. The new system would reduce warehousing costs by £70,000 per annum, but because there will only be one warehouse the costs of shipping goods to customers will rise by £90,000. These figures will not be affected by inflation or tax. The company has a required rate of return of 15 per cent.

(a) What is the Internal Rate of Return on the project?
(b) Should it be accepted?

7. A state-owned telephone company is deciding whether to replace an electro-mechanical exchange with a digital one in a small village. The new exchange would cost £25,000 to buy and install. There would be no net scrap value for the old equipment. The new digital exchange has an expected life of seven years. The old exchange could continue operating for this period.

   The benefit of a digital exchange would be a reduction in maintenance costs. Costs for a digital exchange are negligible. An electro-mechanical exchange requires 50 man hours of labour each year, plus an additional 10 hours for every 100,000 phone calls made or received during the year. Next year the number of calls going through the exchange is expected to be 300,000 and this number is rising at 20,000 per annum. The incremental cost of each man hour of maintenance labour is £22.50 and this is rising at 10 per cent per year. The rate of inflation is 5 per cent per annum.

(a) Calculate the NPV if the required rate of return is 15 per cent.
(b) The government ministry which oversees the telephone company specifies that projects must have a real return (that is, inflation-adjusted return) of 8 per cent. Does the project meet this criterion?

8. Some of the following projects have precursor projects and/or projects with which they are mutually exclusive. All NPVs have been calculated at the company's required rate of return of 18 per cent. Which set of projects should be accepted?

Project	NPV	Precursor projects	Mutually exclusive projects
A	3m	—	G
B	22m	—	C
C	4m	—	B
D	(4m)	—	—
E	2m	D, B	—
F	1m	B	—
G	8m	C	A
H	17m	C, D	—

References and Further Reading

Bierman, H. and Smidt, S. (1984) *The Capital Budgeting Decision*, 6th edn, MacMillan.

Magee, J.F. (1964) 'How to use decision trees in capital investment', *Harvard Business Review*, September–October, pp. 79–96.

Schwab, B. and Lusztig, P. (1969) 'A comparative analysis of the net present value and the benefit cost ratios as measures of the economic desirability of investment', *Journal of Finance*, June, Vol. 24, No. 3, pp. 507–516.

Weingartner, H.M. (1963) *Mathematical Programming and the Analysis of Capital Budgeting Problems*, Prentice Hall.

Weingartner, H.M. (1977) 'Capital rationing: authors in search of a plot', *Journal of Finance*, December, Vol. 32, No. 5, pp. 1403–1431.

Westwick, C.A. and Shohet, P.S.D. (1976) *Investment Appraisal and Inflation*, Institute of Chartered Accountants, Occasional Paper No. 7.

4

The Tax Regime in the UK

Taxation

Chapter 2 has argued that cash flows for appraisal purposes should be
measured after corporate tax but before personal tax. In many countries,
including the US, these two stages in the taxation system operate independently of each other. The corporate tax bill is assessed and paid on the basis
of profits after allowed deductions. Personal taxes are paid by investors on
the dividends they receive and the capital gains that they realise. Companies
may be required to withhold some personal tax on the dividends they pay,
but this is only for administrative convenience. The minority of investors
not liable for personal tax on the dividend can claim back the withheld tax.
The separation of corporate and personal tax is called a 'classical' taxation
system and such a system makes it easy to measure 'after-corporate-tax'
cash flow.

The UK tax system makes it difficult to draw a neat distinction between
these two levels of tax. This system, known as an 'imputation' tax system,
allows part of the tax paid at company level to be counted as meeting part
of the investor's personal tax bill. It substantially meets the criticism that
the 'classical' system involves double taxation of investors, and from this
point of view it has considerable advantages. Unfortunately, it is also more
difficult to analyse.

The system can best be explained by an example. Suppose Candhu plc has
100 million shares outstanding and has earned taxable income of £30 million
in the financial year ending 31 December 1988. The directors are likely to
be able to announce this profit two or three months after the year end and
they will announce the final dividend at the same time. If the dividend is set
at 7.5p per share, an investor holding 1,000 shares will be sent a cheque for
£75. Typically, the cheques will be sent out two or three months after the

announcement. The 7.5p per share that the investor receives is a net dividend. From his point of view, the 7.5p can be regarded as the remaining amount after income tax has been deducted at source. If the tax rate (T) is 25 per cent, the amount of income tax associated with an after tax payment of 7.5p is $7.5(T/1\text{-}T) = 7.5(0.25/0.75) = 2.5$ pence.

The gross amount of the dividends is therefore $7.5 + 2.5 = 10.0$ pence. Of this, 75 per cent is received by the investor as a cheque. The remaining 25 per cent is received as a tax credit. For a standard rate taxpayer this credit just matches his liability and no further money need change hands. A pension fund, however, has no income tax liability and can therefore claim back the 2.5p from the Inland Revenue. A higher rate taxpayer would have to pay an additional amount. The gross dividend can therefore be treated as the dividend before payment of personal income tax.

Although the 2.5p per share (£2.5m in total) paid to the Revenue appears like withholding tax on the gross dividend, that is not its formal title. It is called 'Advance Corporation Tax' (ACT) and counts as partial payment of the company's corporation tax liability. At a corporation tax rate of 35 per cent, total liability for corporation tax is $0.35 \times 30\,\text{M} = £10.5\,\text{M}$. This liability will be negotiated and finally agreed perhaps eight or nine months after the end of the financial year, when the dividend and the associated ACT have already been paid. Of the total corporation tax liability, £2.5m has already been covered by ACT and the company is only required to make a further payment of Mainstream Corporation Tax (MCT) of $10.5 - 2.5 = 8.0$ million pounds.

Several other aspects of the UK system should be noted, although only the main features can be described here in a simplified and truncated form. The maximum amount of ACT that can be offset against corporation tax liability is based on the assumption of full distribution of taxable income. This ensures that companies pay a minimum level of MCT in relation to their taxable income. This aspect of the system is particularly important for companies with large overseas income, where the dividend can be large compared with their taxable UK income.

Interest payments are deducted before the figure for taxable income is struck, but are then liable where appropriate to personal tax as part of the investors' income. In most cases a bank acts as an intermediary between companies and individuals in the debt market. Companies pay interest to banks who, in turn, pay interest to depositors.

Capital Gains Tax is payable on the profit from the disposal of shares at a price above the adjusted purchase price. The adjusted purchase price is the original purchase price increased by the percentage rise in the RPI between purchase and sale. In 1988/9 Capital Gains Tax was payable at the investors' marginal personal tax rate (25 per cent or 40 per cent) on gains above the annual exemption limit of £5,000. It is apparent from this that CGT's bark is worse than its bite. CGT is a postponable tax, and since money has a time value, a tax postponed is a tax alleviated. An investor who makes 10 per cent pre-tax per annum on his investment then sells at the end of one year, pays a 40 per cent tax on his gains and reduces his after-tax return to 6 per cent. An investor who makes 10 per cent pre-tax per annum on his money then sells at the end of 30 years pays 40 per cent tax on his gains and only reduces his after-tax returns to 8.1 per cent, since:

$$(1.081)^{30} = (1.10)^{30} (1 - 0.40)$$

In any year, taxpayers can offset gains on some investments against losses on others. This provision is used with skill to reduce tax. Investors will deliberately sell a security which has performed badly in order to establish a loss and cancel out a gain elsewhere in their portfolio. They may even buy the security back shortly after establishing the loss, a stock market manoeuvre known as 'bed and breakfasting', although this is now limited by avoidance legislation. The inflation adjustment provision also reduces the impact of CGT substantially. With expected inflation at 6 per cent, about 30–40 per cent of the total return on shares might represent compensation for inflation. If so, the effective impact of the tax is reduced by that proportion. For these three reasons, we shall treat CGT in the model that follows as equivalent to a tax of 10 per cent levied each year on gains whether realised or unrealised without inflation adjustment. We shall not distinguish between higher rate and standard rate taxpayers. This rough approximation makes it possible for us to use a much simpler model of the tax system.

The Total Impact of the System

It is not enough to look at individual taxes in isolation. What influences decisions is the total burden of taxation on any business venture. This burden must be measured from the investors' point of view, since the objective of business decisions is to create wealth for shareholders. Taxes that fall on business also fall, indirectly, on investors and should be considered alongside the taxes that bear directly on investors. The way to measure the total burden of the system is on a pocket-to-pocket basis: by looking at the total tax paid on the round trip that starts with an investor putting money into a company and ends with money coming back to him after all taxes have been deducted.

The tax burden on the round trip depends on the route that is taken. There are three routes:

(1) equity rewarded by a 100 per cent payout of profits or dividends;
(2) equity paying no dividend, rewarded by the capital gains produced by retention of profits;
(3) debt rewarded by interest.

For each of these routes, we shall look at the tax paid:

(i) where the company pays MCT on the marginal pound of profit;
(ii) where the company has sufficient tax allowances so that it does not pay MCT.

Table 4.1 assumes that a company has an opportunity to invest in an asset giving a 15 per cent pre-tax return. It is assumed that the writing down allowance available for tax purposes just matches the investment required to maintain the economic value of the asset. The 15 per cent is the profit over and above the cash flow needed to maintain economic value.

Gross Investors and MCT-Paying Companies

Out of the mass of information presented in Table 4.1, we should look first at the most common combination among sizeable UK companies: that is, MCT payers whose dominant shareholders are gross funds. The total tax burden can be calculated for each investment route. For 100 per cent payout equity, gross investors received 13 per cent after all taxes compared with the 15 per cent that the company earned pre-tax. The effective tax rate is therefore $(15 - 13)/15 = 13.3$ per cent. Our assumption that the effective total tax for each of the three investment yields 15 per cent pre-tax was arbitrary, but the effective tax rate of 13.3 per cent is the same whatever return the investment gives.

Table 4.1

| | Equity | | | | Debt | |
| | 100% Payout | | 0% Payout | | | |
	MCT	No MCT	MCT	No MCT	MCT	No MCT
Initial injection						
= Investment	100	100	100	100	100	100
Pre-tax return	15	15	15	15	15	15
Corporation tax						
[ACT + MCT]	5.25	3.75	5.25	—	—	—
After-corporation tax dividend, interest or retention	9.75	11.25	9.75	15	15	15
Tax credit	3.25	3.75	—	—	—	—
After-tax return to gross fund	13	15	9.75	15	15	15
After-tax return to standard rate payer [25%]	9.75	11.25	8.77	13.5	11.25	11.25
After-tax return to 40% income tax payer	7.8	9.0	8.77	13.5	9.0	9.0

The effective total tax for each of the three investment routes is as follows:

Route	Total tax	
Debt	0	Most efficient
Equity with 100 per cent payout	13.3	Intermediate
Equity with 0 per cent payout	35	Least efficient

The next issue is how to use these tax rates in the calculation of an after-tax cash flow. The method recommended in Chapter 2 was to deduct interest to get taxable income; subtract tax at the appropriate corporate rate; and then to add back the interest to get after-tax cash flow. Our analysis of the UK system has shown that the equity tax rate varies with dividend policy. We need to know the company's payout policy, because total tax will vary from 35 per cent with 0 per cent payout to 13.3 per cent with 100 per cent payout. Suppose x per cent of profit is paid out. The effective tax rate (T) is then:

$$T = \frac{x}{100}(0.133) + \frac{100 - x}{100}(0.35)$$

On average, companies pay out about 30 per cent of their income, although this varies greatly. For $x = 30$ per cent, $T = 28.5$ per cent.

An Example

Quaich plc is a medium-sized listed company with 70 per cent of its shares in the hands of pension funds and other tax-exempt institutions. It is profitable and pays mainstream corporation tax. A Quaich subsidiary in the motor parts business is considering setting up a computer database to keep a list of classic cars and car parts for sale. The incremental cost of this project will be the purchase of a computer and the labour involved and a range of overhead items including the costs of space, management supervision, marketing, etc. The computer is the only significant item of capital cost, and is expected to have a five-year life, with a scrap value of £15,000 at the end. Quaich management does not expect the current level of interest in classical cars to be long-lasting and will therefore evaluate the project over a five-year horizon. Revenues are expected to be £30,000 per annum; the computer will cost £80,000; and direct labour costs plus all incremental overhead items will be £12,000 per annum.

To calculate the after-tax cash flow from this project, we need to know Quaich's debt policy and payout policy. Suppose that Quaich finances assets like the computer with 60 per cent equity and 40 per cent debt (at 12 per cent interest), and that Quaich pays out dividends based on 28 per cent of its income. The cash flow calculation is shown in Table 4.2.

Notice that the cash flow of a project is improved the more it is financed

Table 4.2

	Now	Year 1	Year 2	Year 3	Year 4	Year 5	Year 6
Initial outlay and scrap value	(80,000)						15,000
Revenue		30,000	30,000	30,000	30,000	30,000	
Costs		12,000	12,000	12,000	12,000	12,000	
Writing down allowance		20,000	15,000	11,250	8,437	9,117[b]	
Debt[a]	32,000	24,000	18,000	13,500	10,125	7,594	
Interest		3,840	2,880	2,160	1,620	1,245	
Taxable income		(5,840)	120	4,590	7,943	7,668	
Tax at 29 per cent[c]			1,694	(35)	(1,331)	(2,303)	(2,224)
After-tax cash flow	(80,000)	18,000	19,694	17,955	16,669	30,697	(2,224)

Notes: (a) Debt in each year is 40 per cent of the book value of the computer at the beginning of the year.
(b) This is the WDA of £6,328 allowable in year 5, plus 70 per cent of the £3,984 that remains to be written off in future years. £3,984 is the difference between the book value of the computer at the time it is scrapped (£18,984) and the price received for it (£15,000). The 70 per cent figure takes account of the fact that the depreciation would in practice be spread over many future years.
(c) Twenty-nine per cent is the appropriate corporate tax rate on equity with a 28 per cent dividend payout.

by debt and the more generous the dividend payout policy of the company. Because of the complex nature of the UK tax system, it has been impossible to analyse a project entirely independently of financing decisions. However, project appraisal can still be carried out at division or subsidiary level, so long as the divisions are told:

(1) the proportion of debt used in financing the different categories of assets;

(2) the dividend payout policy, and the resulting effective tax rate on equity.

Since debt policy and payout policy affect the attractiveness of investments, it may be wondered why companies typically use only a modest proportion of debt and restrict their dividends to a small proportion of earnings. Our analysis suggests that their shareholders would benefit from policy changes. These are important but controversial topics in the theory of finance. The specialised focus of this book precludes full discussion. However, it is worth noting that the financial policies of many large companies at present appear to be non-optimal. Perhaps the adjustment of financial policy to the current tax system is not yet complete.

Non-MCT-Paying Companies/Gross Investors

The circumstances under which project income will be fully protected against MCT are restrictive. This will only happen if the company will not be paying MCT, with or without the project, into the indefinite future. Not only is this a rare circumstance, it is also a circumstance that corporate finance executives work actively to forestall. A company that is not paying MCT has unused tax allowances. If this is a long-term situation, it implies that tax allowances are going to remain unused for a long time. This is inefficient: tax allowances are worth more if they are used promptly, and financial managers are going to look for ways, through mergers and business reorganisations for example, to ensure that this happens.

If project income is fully sheltered from MCT, then corporation tax can be omitted from the calculations altogether because ACT is effectively an investor tax. In the Quaich example, the cash flow calculation would simply be as shown in Table 4.3.

Table 4.3

	Now	Year 1	Year 2	Year 3	Year 4	Year 5	Year 6
Capital items	(80,000)						15,000
Revenue		30,000	30,000	30,000	30,000	30,000	30,000
Cost		(12,000)	(12,000)	(12,000)	(12,000)	(12,000)	(12,000)
Cash flow	(80,000)	18,000	18,000	18,000	18,000	18,000	33,000

A more common situation is that the company is temporarily not paying MCT. Perhaps it expects to be free for the next two years. Notice that it would be wrong in this case to ignore the tax liability for the first two years but to bring it in for later years. Even in the first two years, if the project is generating taxable income, it is using up part of the company's stock of unused allowances. That means that the company will pay tax in year three on income unrelated to the project that would otherwise have been sheltered. The tax on the first two years of operations is not really avoided: it is only postponed. A fully correct approach would calculate the tax liabilities in the first two years and move them across to year three. As an approximation, it would be much better to ignore the temporary absence of MCT, and treat each year's income as taxable in the normal way, than to ignore tax liability in two years and only allow for tax on the income in the third and subsequent years.

Investors' Taxes

So long as the firm's objective is the creation of market value for its investors, investor or personal taxes can be ignored in the analysis as we have already shown in Chapter 2. There may be cases, however, where a company has shareholders whose tax position is out of line with that of the majority of investors in the market. One example would be a family-controlled firm in an environment where gross funds are the dominant investors on the market. If the family firm is a long-term investor, it may be interested in the present value of its after-tax income, and decisions that maximise this may *not* be the ones that maximise market value. The solution in this special case would be to measure incremental cash flow after personal taxes and calculate an NPV of this using a required rate of return that reflected the after-tax opportunity cost to the family of providing the investment funds. It would be naive, though, to think of the shareholder in family firms as facing particularly harsh levels of personal taxation. Family trusts and other devices tend to bring them into line with other investors, most of whom are able to benefit from advantageous tax treatment.

Overseas Tax for UK Companies

This is a highly complex and detailed issue, and we can only comment here on some of the general principles involved.

Foreign countries operate a wide variety of corporate fiscal regimes. Most tend to be classical rather than imputation systems, but even among the classical systems there are wide differences in the rates of tax and the generosity of the allowances for depreciation, working capital needs, self-insurance, etc. that can be deducted in the calculation of taxable income. The effective burden imposed by any tax system can only be discovered by careful analysis of the fine points of the tax code and the precedents relating to its application.

UK-owned subsidiaries operating overseas may well find that they pay tax both on the profits that they generate locally and on any dividends that they remit to their UK parent. Sometimes exchange controls prevent the repatriation of profits earned in the host country and this, of course, means that quoted exchange rates are not applicable when appraising new projects which will generate blocked revenues.

The UK has double taxation agreements with most developed non-communist nations. The general tenor of these agreements is that UK companies are liable to UK tax on all their worldwide earnings but that tax paid to foreign governments is deducted from the final UK tax payments. Where profits have been generated in a low-rate 'tax haven' overseas, the UK revenue authorities will collect the difference between UK rates and overseas rates. Where taxes have been paid overseas at a higher rate than in the UK the excess cannot be offset against tax due on the company's UK operations.

The ACT that arises when a UK company pays dividends can only be offset against UK corporation tax liability. A company operating success-fully internationally but with insufficient taxable income in the UK will pay 'unrelieved' ACT when it pays a dividend. There is a tax inefficiency involved when 'unrelieved' ACT is paid, and if the situation seems likely to continue a company would try to acquire, by merger or otherwise, sufficient UK earnings to be able to use the ACT as a tax deduction.

The problem that concerns us here is to define after-tax cash flow for projects that will generate taxable profits overseas. There are no new principles involved here, but it is clear from our brief discussion of interna-tional taxation that the calculation may involve overseas tax rates on corporate income and dividends, UK tax rates, and the availability of UK taxable income to relieve the ACT on UK dividends paid out of overseas income.

Study Questions

1. Magnox plc has an average payout ratio of 25 per cent, the rate of mainstream corporation tax is 35 per cent and the amount payable in advance corporation tax is 25 per cent of the gross dividend. The standard rate of income tax is also 25 per cent. What is the effective rate of corporate tax that should be applied in calculating after-tax cash flows? How would this rate change if the 25 per cent income tax/ACT rate was lowered to 15 per cent?

2. Harrington plc has an average payout ratio of 35 per cent. The mainstream corporation tax rate is 40 per cent and the standard rate of income tax is 35 per cent. The amount of ACT payable is 54 per cent of the net dividend. What is the effective rate of corporate tax for this company? How would this rate change if the payout ratio was raised to 50 per cent?

3. The Finance Director of Mallstorm plc uses some of the company's cash to buy assets which he leases to third parties. By doing this he acquires the writing-down allowances associated with these assets and as a result Mallstorm, which is a profitable company in its own right, pays negligible amounts in mainstream corporation tax. How should these leasing deals affect the way the Mallstorm calculates the after-tax cash flow for its own investment projects?

4. Explain how the calculation of after-tax cash flows would be affected if the UK readopted a classical system and company tax at 35 per cent were paid on all taxable company profits and, in addition, income tax were paid by investors on gross dividends received.

References and Further Reading

Institute for Fiscal Studies (1978) *The Structure and Reform of Direct Taxation*, The Meade Report, London.

Kay, J.A. and King, M.A. (1980) *The British Tax System*, Oxford University Press.

Miller, M.H. (1977) 'Debt and taxes', *Journal of Finance*, May, Vol. 32, No. 2, pp. 261–275.

5

Required Rates of Return

In the financial markets, money has a price. For risk-free fully liquid loans and deposits, this price is the prevailing interest rate. Where there is risk or appraisal costs or transactions costs, the price of money will be higher.

Company management acts in the interests of shareholders. The basic question in the appraisal process is whether the project will give a return that is at least as good as that which the shareholders could have got if they had taken their money elsewhere and backed other projects with comparable risk, appraisal costs, etc. In the economist's language, an acceptable project is one which returns something more than the opportunity cost of the funds it uses.

Assessing the market's cost of funds for a particular project is a little like estimating the market price of a house. You would start by identifying the key elements which affect house prices — the total floor area, the size of garden, whether there is central heating and double glazing, etc. Next, you would estimate how each of these features contributes to price to generate a pricing formula. Finally, you would measure and inspect the house in question and put the results into the formula to get a price. In the case of a house, of course, you can take a short cut by putting the house up for auction. Businesses, however, do not become successful by auctioning off their business opportunities, so that project appraisal involves making an inference about the opportunity cost of funds rather than observing the cost directly in the market.

Setting the required rate of return is therefore a three-part process:

(1) Identify the factors that affect returns in the financial markets.

(2) Measure how each factor affects the return.

(3) Assess the project to see how it scores for each of the factors and hence calculate the required return.

The first two of these stages require an analysis of how financial markets evaluate risky assets. The main category of risky assets which are traded in the market is, of course, company shares, also known as equities. We shall start by considering the returns that they offer, although our ultimate objective is to identify the cost of funds for particular projects, not whole companies.

The Cost of Equity

Rewarding the shareholders is a cost to the company, but to the shareholders it is a return. The cost of equity from the company's viewpoint is the same thing as the return on equity to the shareholders so long as taxation is treated consistently. We are interested in these costs and returns on a forward-looking basis, which means we are concerned with expectations about the future rather than historical experience. This makes the problem harder. How can we measure the return that investors are expecting from a particular company's shares? It is not an easy task and there are two main approaches.

(1) The Dividend–Growth Model

The model starts with a dividend-based equation for the value of a share. The return the investor receives is the rate (K) at which the discounted value of the future dividends to be paid on a share $(D_1, D_2, \ldots)$ equals the current market price of the share (P). K is therefore the IRR on the cash flows from the shareholder's investment if he buys the share now and holds it indefinitely. If the dividend is paid annually and the next dividend is due in one year, then:

$$P = \frac{D_1}{1 + K} + \frac{D_2}{(1 + K)^2} + \ldots + \frac{D_i}{(1 + K)^i} + \ldots$$

In its simpler form, the model assumes that the company will increase its dividend per share at a constant annual rate, g, forever, so that:

$$D_i = D_1(1 + g)^{i-1}$$

The equation then becomes:

$$P = \frac{D_1}{1 + K} + \frac{D_1(1 + g)}{(1 + K)^2} + \frac{D_1(1 + g)^2}{(1 + K)^3} + \ldots + \frac{D_1(1 + g)^{i-1}}{(1 + K)^i} + \ldots$$

The RHS is a geometric series which has a finite sum so long as $g < K$. Using the standard formula for the sum of a geometric series the equation becomes:

$$P = \frac{D_1}{K - g}$$

Our interest is in K, the return to the investor, and we assume that the other variables are known. Rearranging the equation to give an expression for K produces:

$$K = \frac{D_1}{P} + g$$

This is a prominent formula in most textbooks. g is often measured from the company's historic records. An illustration of its use would be as follows:

An Example

Nordec plc paid gross dividends per share of 3.7p in 1978 and is expected to pay 8.0p this year (1988). The company's share price is now 125p and the company's past growth rate is expected to continue. Calculate Nordec's cost of equity.

Answer

Nordec's dividends have grown by $8.0/3.7 = 2.16$ times over the past 10 years. The annual rate is found by solving:

$$(1 + g)^{10} = 2.16$$

which gives $g = 0.08 = 8$ per cent.
The cost of equity capital is then calculated as:

$$K = \frac{D_1}{P} + g = \frac{8}{125} + 0.08 = 0.144 = 14.4\%$$

One variation of this method is to use earnings per share rather than dividends per share to estimate company growth on the grounds that earnings are the best measure of the company's progress, and dividends can vary with the financial policy of the directors or in response to changes in the tax system. The other side of the argument is that earnings are subject to fluctuations due to short-term factors, while dividends are set by the directors based on their view of the long-run sustainable prospects for the firm.

One danger in using the $D_1/P + g$ formula is that the cost of equity capital seems to depend on the generosity of dividend policy. This is not so.

If a firm decides to pay out more in dividends, it will have to plough back less. A fall in plough-back will reduce the future growth rate of earnings or dividends per share. Changes in D_1/P will therefore be associated with offsetting changes in g and there is no clear logical relationship between dividend policy and cost of capital.

In practice there are two major weaknesses in the dividend growth model. Firstly, there is a considerable body of academic research, stemming from work by Rayner and Little (1966), which suggests that growth in company earnings (and largely in dividends too) is 'higgledy-piggledy' rather than stable. This indicates that values of g calculated from historic data will have very little predictive value and will not be the good measure of the current investor estimate of future growth that the formula requires. Indeed, the mechanical use of historic data can give very foolish results: a company in financial difficulty which has cut its dividend may appear to have a negative cost of equity capital. In fact, of course, investors would require a substantial premium over market interest rates to persuade them to invest in such a troubled company, and the true cost of equity capital for such a company is likely to be rather higher than that for companies with sound finances and a record of growth.

For this reason it is common to look to analysts in stockbrokers or other financial institutions to provide an estimate of g. Such organisations often carry out appraisals of company prospects and are close to investors whose expectations underly the cost of equity; they are therefore in a relatively good position to provide an answer. The difficulty is that their analysis is probably too sophisticated to suggest that the company will have a constant long-run rate of growth. Indeed, the assumption that one number can summarise the whole of a firm's growth potential is the second major weakness in the model.

Financial analysts often find it more realistic to use a two-stage model which assumes that the dividend will grow at g_1 until the dividend is paid $n + 1$ years from now, and at g_2 thereafter. In this case, we must solve the following equation for K, with all the other variables known:

$$P = \frac{D_1}{1 + K} + \frac{D_1(1 + g_1)}{(1 + K)^2} + \cdots + \frac{D_1(1 + g_1)^n}{(1 + K)^{n+1}}$$
$$+ \frac{D_1(1 + g_1)^n(1 + g_2)}{(1 + K)^{n+2}} + \cdots + \frac{D_1(1 + g_1)^n(1 + g_2)^i}{(1 + K)^{n+i+1}} + \cdots$$

This expression has a finite sum so long as $g_2 < K$; the expression can be simplified to:

$$\frac{P}{D_1} = \frac{1}{K - g_1} - \left[\frac{1}{K - g_1} - \frac{1}{K - g_2}\right]\left[\frac{1 + g_i}{1 + K}\right]^n$$

This equation can be solved without difficulty by a trial and error procedure on a spreadsheet. As an illustration of this formula, if:

$$P \; = \; 229\text{p}$$

$$D \; = \; 14\text{p}$$

$$g_1 \; = \; 20\% \; = \; 0.20$$

$$g_2 \; = \; 7\% \; = \; 0.07$$

$$n \; = \; 4 \text{ years}$$

then it will be found that the cost of equity, K, is 16 per cent.

With modification, therefore, the dividend–growth model is of practical value. But we should also consider an alternative approach to measuring the cost of equity.

(2) The Capital Asset Pricing Model (CAPM)

This is a theoretical approach to estimating the returns on shares which was developed in the 1960s. It starts from a model of the risk in investing in shares that was developed by Sharpe (1964). This model, called the market model, assumes that share prices are subject to two different kinds of risk:

1. Market or systematic risk   The share goes up or down with movements of the market as a whole measured by a broadly based market index. The measure of market risk for any share is called its β coefficient. A β of 1.5 would mean that, if the market as a whole went up by an extra 1 per cent, we would expect this share to go up by an extra 1.5 per cent. These βs hold for downward movements in the market as well as rises, so if the market unexpectedly fell 1 per cent the share would be likely to fall 1.5 per cent.

A share with a β of 1.5 would be an 'aggressive' holding, attractive to investors who expected the market to rise. A share with a β of 0.5 would be a defensive stock, which would fall less than the market index if the market as a whole declined. Clearly, if the market index rises 1 per cent this must mean that, subject to suitable weighting, the average share has risen 1 per cent. This tells us that, by definition, the average β must be 1.

2. Specific or unsystematic risk   This covers the remainder of the risk, where shares go up and down for reasons unique to themselves. In any time period, shares will be affected by both systematic and unsystematic factors.

In mathematical terms, the market model states that:

$$\tilde{R}_{it} \; = \; \alpha_i + B_i \tilde{R}_{Mt} + \tilde{E}_{it}$$

where:

$\tilde{R}_{it}$ is the uncertain (hence the $\sim$ superscript) return on the ith share in the tth time period.

α_i is the constant element in the return. It varies from share to share, but for any particular share it will remain constant over time.

β_i has already been explained. Like α, the model assumes that β is a constant for each share.

$\tilde{R}_{Mt}$ the uncertain return on the market as a whole in time period t.

$\tilde{E}_{it}$ the uncertain element of specific risk for the ith share in the tth period. The average value of E_{it} will be zero, because any constant trend upwards or downwards will be incorporated in α_i. However, some shares will have more specific risk than others, and this will be measured by σ_{Ei}, the standard deviation of $\tilde{E}_{it}$.

Share prices respond to unexpected events in the real world: political changes, technological breakthroughs, fads and fashions. Because these cannot be forecast, share prices will move in unpredictable ways, and they can be modelled as if price changes were random numbers generated by chance. Indeed, the market model effectively says that the stock market can be modelled by rolling dice. First, dice would be rolled to simulate the movement of the market as a whole, to which individual share movements would be linked by their β coefficients. Then other dice would be rolled to simulate the unsystematic price movements for each share. This does *not* imply that share price movements are actually random, meaningless events unrelated to real economic developments. The claim is simply that they can be modelled by random processes.

The breakdown of risk into two components is particularly important when we consider that investors hold portfolios of shares. They spread their money across a range of different companies rather than putting all their financial eggs in one basket.

The market risk of a portfolio can be defined as the β of the portfolio, since a portfolio has a return that is linked to the market just like a share. The β of a portfolio is just the average of the βs of the shares in it, weighted by the proportion of the total value of the portfolio in each share.

The specific risk of a portfolio can be almost completely diversified away. It would not be quite true to say that the specific risks of the different shares in the portfolio cancel out, but the total level of specific risk in the portfolio does fall dramatically as the funds are spread over a larger number of shares. Most specific risk will have gone if the money is equally split between a dozen shares. Almost all of it will have gone if the funds are split between fifty.

The argument only confirms what most people know by instinct: diversification of investments makes very good sense. And most investors, either by constructing their own portfolios or by putting their money into investment and unit trusts, benefit from it. The consequences are paradoxical. Specific risk does not hurt investors because they diversify it away, and therefore investors do not require any extra expected return from a share to compensate for extra specific risk. In this sense, specific risk is not priced. The only risk that really counts is market risk: it cannot be diversified away. Investors do not like risk, so shares with a higher β must offer a higher return. If we specify that:

(a) the return on a share is linearly related to its β;

(b) a share with $\beta = 0$ has no risk premium in its expected return, which must equal the risk-free interest rate (R_f);

(c) a share with $\beta = 1$ has average risk and must offer average expected return, i.e. the expected return on the market portfolio, written as $\bar{R}_m$;

then the relationship between the risk of a share and the expected return on a share $(\bar{R}_i)$ must be:

$$\bar{R}_i = R_f + \beta_i[\bar{R}_m - R_f]$$

Only the systematic risk β_i appears in this equation. Unsystematic risk does not affect returns. This equation is known as the Capital Asset Pricing Model (CAPM) and is the basic equation for our second method of calculating the cost of equity capital. There are two obvious questions about this theoretically devised formula: is it true? and how can it be applied in practice?

The market model itself is only an approximation. Shares in the same industry often move together and this fact is not captured by the model. But it hardly matters because industry–group risk, like specific risk, can be diversified away and would not be priced.

A more serious problem is that the βs are only modestly stable over time. To measure β from the past record of share price movements requires several years of data. When it has been measured, its value as a predictor of β in the future is fair. There is a tendency for high βs and low βs to persist, but there are also cases of βs that change dramatically over time.

The proposition that specific risk is unpriced is very hard to prove because of the statistical difficulties involved in the tests. Since there is strong evidence that investors do diversify specific risk out of their portfolios, the claim that specific risk is unpriced does, at least, seem highly credible.

There is one final problem. Betas in the UK have traditionally been measured against the UK market as a whole as measured by, for example, the FT Actuaries All-Share Index. The logic of this is that the FT Actuaries Index represents the whole universe of stock market investments available to the UK investor. If this was ever true, perhaps in the era of exchange controls, it is certainly not true now. International portfolio investment has grown rapidly in the 1980s. Should βs be measured against an index of world investment opportunities? At present, the calculations are merely based on national markets.

Applying the Theory

The risk-free rate is easily observable. It is usually taken as the rate on three-month Treasury Bills. A longer-term rate is justified, however, when a required return for longer-term projects is being calculated.

Table 5.1

Industry	Industry $\beta(\beta_I)$
Contracting, construction	1.06
Electrical and electronic engineering	1.13
Mechanical engineering	0.97
Metals	1.08
Motors and vehicles	1.05
Brewers and distillers	0.94
Food manufacture	0.92
Retailing	0.94
Printing and publishing	0.91
Textiles	1.14
Chemicals	0.98
Shipping and transport	0.96
Oil	0.90
Property	0.76

Source: London Business School Risk Measurement Service, 1987.

Betas are calculated for almost all significant UK companies and published by the London Business School in its quarterly 'Risk Measurement Service'. Because of the uncertainty surrounding calculations of β for individual companies, it seems more practical to look at the typical βs for the different industry sectors. Table 5.1 shows the industry βs. Notice that none of the βs departs very far from 1. Generally, it is capital goods industries which have the highest βs. This is not surprising, because they are particularly sensitive to the swings of the economic cycle. The low β industries, generally, are those involved in supplying the necessary consumables of life: food, beer, etc.

The final element in the formula is $\bar{R}_m - R_f$ which is usually described as the risk premium on the market. It is the amount by which the return on shares is expected to exceed R_f. This has been estimated for the UK at 9 per cent, taking the historic average over a 60-year period (Dimson and Brealey, 1978); for 1919–1984 a similar estimate, 9.15 per cent, has been made by Allen, Day, Kwiatkowski and Hirst (1986). This rate matches the 8.8 per cent risk premium on shares in the US estimated on a similar long-term basis by Ibbotson and Sinquefield (1976).

Since 9 per cent is a key number in the calculation of required returns, it is worth considering how robust and accurate an estimate it is likely to be. It will not be greatly affected by sudden market movements. The spectacular 30 per cent fall in the stock market in October 1987 will only change the long-term estimate by about 0.6 per cent.

The standard deviation of annual returns has been approximately 25 per cent, and on this basis the standard deviation of the annual average over a 60-year period is $25/\sqrt{60} = 3.2$ per cent. This suggests that there is, very roughly, a one-in-six chance that the true risk premium is at or above 12 per cent (one standard deviation above the mean) and a one-in-six chance that it is at or below 6 per cent.

The author's guess is that the last 60 years have been a period in which, overall, the performance of the stock market has exceeded expectations. There has been victory in a world war, a significant rise in popular support for the capitalist system, and the development of a system of pension provision which has put many billions of pounds of long-term money into the stock market. Nine per cent may, therefore, be an overestimate of the expected risk premium on shares but it is unlikely to be more than 3 per cent above the true figure.

In the examples that follow, we shall continue to use the 9 per cent estimate, but it is worth remembering that there is a serious case for using a figure that might be significantly lower.

The Company Size Effect

In recent years, one major limitation of CAPM has become apparent. The historic evidence seems to show that equity returns are higher on shares of small companies. Here, size is measured in terms of the total market value of the company's shares. For the UK, the phenomenon has been measured by Dimson and Marsh (1984). Smoothing their findings to a considerable extent, they would appear to justify the size premia in equity returns shown in Table 5.2.

The discovery of the size effect was an unexpected result of academic studies of the stock market. It had not been predicted and there is no clear theoretical explanation for it. It may well be associated with economies of scale in the production of the information about a company needed to create a liquid market in its shares. Companies with a capitalisation of above £25m are likely to be of interest to institutional shareholders and are therefore likely to be well followed by stockbrokers. Smaller companies are perhaps less well served.

The calculation of the historic risk premium on shares in the section

Table 5.2

Size (equity capitalisation, £m)	Size premium
Over 25m	0
12m–25m	+1%
6m–12m	+2%
3m–6m	+3%
Below 3m	+4% or above

above is dominated by returns from large companies. So the size adjustment means higher returns for small companies, not lower returns for larger ones.

These figures do not mean that the financial markets have a built-in bias against small companies. What the small firm loses in higher equity cost it may well win back through lower overheads and less internal bureaucracy.

Project Risk

We have already argued that the pricing of risk in the financial markets is complex. Ideally, we would like to apply the CAPM directly to an individual project. This would involve calculating a 'project β'. In appendices to this chapter, we shall look at two techniques that take this approach.

Most businesses will find the techniques difficult to apply because of the information required as an input. In the main body of this chapter we shall take a very simple approach, which has proved workable in the business environment. All projects are placed in one of four risk categories and the risk premium is adjusted according to the following schedule:

Project category	Adjustment factor
Fixed cost reduction	60%
Variable cost reduction	85%
Capacity expansion	115%
Initial venture in new business area	140% and up

Fixed cost reduction is the least risky category because the benefits of the project will come through whether the business as a whole prospers or not. Variable cost reduction is another category involving below-average risk. Most equipment replacement/plant modernisation projects fall into this category. Capacity expansion slightly raises the risk level of the firm and therefore has a positive adjustment factor. More capacity, other things being equal, means a greater risk that capacity will exceed demand and that plant will be idle. The adjustment for ventures in new business areas is discretionary. Some ventures, particularly ones with strong links to the existing business, may have limited risk. Entry into completely unproven markets unrelated to the company's existing strengths may merit a substantially higher adjustment factor.

Required Rate of Return for a Project

The expected return on the equity for any industry can be calculated from the CAPM formula. It is:

$$R_f + [B_i \times 0.09]$$

We need to adjust this to get the expected return on the whole pool of funds which is used for investments, both debt and equity. The cost of debt is the risk-free rate. If the proportion of debt in the industry's financial pool is g, the Industry Base Return is:

$$g.R_f + (1 - g)[R_f + (B_i \times 0.09)] = R_f + (1 - g)(B_i \times 0.09)$$

and hence the basic risk premium for an industry is:

$$(1 - g)(B_i \times 0.09).$$

Different industries have different levels of gearing. Estimates of basic risk premia for a number of industries are given in Table 5.3.

The required return for any project, then, is the sum of four components. It is:

Risk-free Rate + (Basic Industry Risk Premium) × Project Risk

Adjustment Factor + Company Size Adjustment Factor

Two points about the formula are worth noting. First, project gearing does not appear in the formula. Debt associated with the project affects the cash flow, but the required return is based, mainly, on an assessment of the project's risk. The two elements will be linked, but only loosely. There will be a tendency for projects with lower risk to have more debt capacity, but debt will perhaps be associated even more closely with securable assets.

Secondly, the company size adjustment is added to the required return, not just to the equity component. This seems reasonable, since both debt

Table 5.3

Industry	Industry β (β_I)	$g(\%)$	Industry premium $(1 - g)(B_I \times 9)\%$
Contracting, construction	1.06	26.7	7.0
Electrical and electronic engineering	1.13	24.0	7.7
Mechanical engineering	0.97	26.1	6.5
Metals	1.08	23.8	7.4
Motors and vehicles	1.05	34.5	6.2
Brewers and distillers	0.94	20.2	6.8
Food manufacture	0.92	27.8	6.0
Retailing	0.94	27.4	6.1
Printing and publishing	0.91	30.5	5.7
Textiles	1.14	28.7	7.3
Chemicals	0.98	32.0	6.0
Shipping and transport	0.96	39.5	5.2
Oil	0.90	39.8	4.9
Property	0.76	32.3	4.6

Sources: London Business School Risk Measurement Service; *Business Monitor M4.*

and equity tend to be more expensive for smaller firms and since the complication of adjusting debt and equity separately is avoided. It means that the risk-free rate in the formula is the rate for the larger companies and the UK government, and is best measured in the market for government securities. If there is a major difference between the interest rate on long- and short-term government securities, then it would be appropriate to match the interest rate to the life of the project. The fact that most borrowing by smaller companies is at a rate significantly above base rate is taken into account in the company size adjustment factor. Small companies do not have to use a higher risk-free rate. The use of this method of setting the required return is best illustrated by an example.

An Example

Morley plc is a modest sized company (Market Cap. £20m) in an industry with a β of 1.15 and an average gearing of 20 per cent. The company proposes to invest in a computerised stock control and ordering system. The current risk free interest rate is 8 per cent. What is the required rate of return for this project?

Answer

The basic risk premium for the industry, in this case, is:

$$(1 - 0.20)(1.15 \times 0.09) = 8.3\%$$

The formula for required return is:

Risk-free Rate + Basic Industry Risk Premium × Project Risk Adjustment Factor + Company Size Adjustment Factor

In this case the project cuts variable costs so the PRAF is 0.85. The CSAF is 1 per cent, so the formula translates to:

$$8\% + 8.3\% \times 0.85 + 1\% = 16.1\%$$

The selection of a required return is one of the most controversial topics in capital budgeting. The method explained here is intended to strike a balance between incorporating modern theories and practicability. The three appendices that follow this chapter explain three established alternative approaches.

Required Returns for International Projects

Adjustment in the required return is necessary when cash flows are measured in currencies other than sterling. The simplest case is where the whole project is located in one overseas country and all the cash flows are in the currency of that country. An example would be a UK construction company appraising a residential development in the south of Spain. Here cash flows would be in pesetas and the required return formula would use the risk-free rate in pesetas, quoted on the Madrid financial markets, instead of the sterling rate.

The question of adjusting the industry risk factor is more controversial. The Spanish construction industry might be regarded as quite different from the British One, and deserving of a separate measure of industry risk. Much of this risk which relates particularly to the relative performance of the Spanish economy and financial markets would be specific risk from the point of UK investors with their funds in the UK market. This diversification effect would suggest that the overseas project should be assigned a lower risk adjustment than normal. On the other hand, the Spanish project will bring currency risks (some of which might be hedged) and our basic formula is rather parochial in measuring all risks against the baseline of the UK market. If a broader picture were taken, and risk were measured in a global rather than a national context, balance of systematic and unsystematic risk for Spanish construction projects would probably be similar to that for British projects, and the justification for a lower risk adjustment factor would disappear.

Better practical models for risk adjustment when appraising international projects may well be developed in the future. The recommendation here is that only the risk-free rate should be changed.

The other case to consider is when a project produces part of its cash flow in foreign currencies. Here the analyst has a choice. One approach would be to calculate the NPV for each currency component separately, using the appropriate risk-free rate in the formula when evaluating each currency. The total NPV of the project is the sum of the NPVs of the different currency components. The alternative is to convert all future cash flows into sterling before converting them into present value. In doing this, it is important to remember that exchange rates are not fixed and that it is not sensible to assume that the exchange rates prevailing today will continue in the future. Expected exchange rates at specific dates in the future can be calculated from information available today. They are called forward exchange rates.

Consider a business that knows it will receive $1 million in one year's time. What exchange rate should be used to convert this into a sterling amount also to be received in one year? The sterling interest rate is 12 per cent, the dollar rate 8 per cent, and the current exchange rate is $1.70 = £1.00. The conversion into sterling can be arranged now even though the money will not be received for a year. The business can borrow $1,000,000/1.08 = $925,926 now, knowing that the $1 million would exactly repay the loan, with interest, in one year. This is converted to sterling at the current rate to give £925,926/1.70 = £544,662 and this money is invested at the sterling rate for a year. At the end of that line the proceeds are £544,662 (1.12) = £610,022. Effectively, then, \$1 million due in one year has been converted to £610,022 due in one year at an effective exchange rate of 1,000,000/610,022 = 1.64 \$ per £. This is the one-year forward exchange rate and it clearly depends on the current exchange rate and interest rates in the two countries.

In general, if E_c is the current exchange rate (in units of foreign currency per pound), $E_f(n)$ is the forward exchange rate for n years hence, and R_s and R_o are the risk-free interest rates in sterling and the overseas currency respectively, then:

$$E_f(n) = E_c \frac{(1 + R_o)^n}{(1 + R_s)^n}$$

This formula provides the exchange rates at which future foreign currency receipts can be converted to equivalent future sterling receipts. Currencies which are likely to lose value against sterling will have to offer higher interest rates as compensation, so that this formula automatically warns a business when a project will give its cash flow in a depreciating currency and makes the necessary adjustment.

It can readily be seen that the two alternative approaches to projects with mixed currency proceeds will give exactly the same result. It is a matter of convenience whether the different currency streams are converted separately to NPV or whether forward exchange rates are used.

Note that cash flow for overseas projects would normally be measured to and from the overseas subsidiary in the same way that they would be measured for a domestic subsidiary. It is not recommended to look only at the cash flows of the parent company. The return, and risk, at the parent level will be heavily influenced by the way the subsidiary is financed, and our objective is to assess the merit of the project rather than the associated financing decisions. Our analysis assumes free convertibility of currencies. If there are limitations on the repatriation of overseas profits, then it may be necessary to measure cash flows at the level of the parent. In these circumstances the risk associated with the cash flow is likely to be high and the required rate of return will need to be adjusted accordingly.

Appendix I: The Weighted Average Cost of Capital (WACC)

This can be regarded as the traditional approach to setting a required rate of return and is recommended in many texts. WACC is defined as:

$$\frac{E}{D + E} R_E + \frac{D}{D + E} R_D(1 - T)$$

D and E are the debt and equity in the company's capital structure. Texts differ as to whether they should be measured at book value or market value, with strong arguments on both sides. Book value may be unrelated to real economic value. The market value of equity may include the prospective value of projects that have not yet started. The author prefers book value. T is the effective rate of corporate tax. Since interest is tax-deductible, it only costs the shareholders $R_D(1 - T)$ of after-corporate-tax income to pay interest of R_D.

There are, therefore, two main differences between the WACC method and the method recommended earlier:

(1) WACC uses the same required rate of return for all of a company's projects. Although this has the advantage of simplicity, it completely ignores factors that might make one project cheaper to fund than another, such as company size and project risk. WACC also uses the same gearing for all projects, whereas we have argued that different projects have different debt capacity, and the analysis adjusted accordingly. WACC does not have this flexibility. WACC is therefore biased in favour of investments in new ventures, research and development, etc. and against more mundane cost reduction projects.

(2) WACC uses the after tax cost of debt $(R_D(1 - T))$ in the calculations. The justification for this is that the WACC method measures cash flow in a different way. It was stressed in Chapter 2 that the required rate of return varies with the point at which cash flow is measured.

WACC measures cash flow after deducting corporate tax on *both* taxable income and on incremental interest, i.e. on all the 'operating income' from the project. It therefore understates cash flow because it deducts more tax than will actually be paid. It compensates for the lower cash flow by setting a lower required rate of return using $R_D(1 - T)$ instead of R_D.

An Example

A project involves the purchase of equipment at a price of £50,000 which will produce incremental revenue of £20,000 per annum for the next four years. The equipment will be valueless at the end of four years. The company will use 30 per cent debt to finance this project. Thirty per cent is also the proportion of debt in the financial structure of the whole company. For simplicity, we use straight line depreciation as an allowable deduction for tax purposes. The cost of equity is 16 per cent, the cost of debt 10 per cent and the rate of corporate tax is 30 per cent. Calculate NPV using both the WACC approach (allowing for tax-deductibility of interest in the required return, not the cash flow) and the recommended method (where the allowance is made in the cash flow).

Table 5.4

Year	0	1	2	3	4
Initial outlay	(50,000)				
Incremental revenue		20,000	20,000	20,000	20,000
Depreciation		12,500	12,500	12,500	12,500
Interest at 10 per cent		1,500	1,125	750	375
Incremental taxable income		6,000	6,375	6,750	7,125
Tax		1,800	1,912	2,025	2,137
After-tax cash flow		18,200	18,088	17,975	17,863

This gives an NPV of:

$$-50,000 + \frac{18,200}{1.142} + \frac{17,975}{(1.142)^2} + \frac{17,975}{(1.142)^3} + \frac{17,863}{(1.142)^4} = 2,378$$

Answer 1: Recommended Method

To make the two approaches comparable, we use a weighted average approach to required return, using R_D, not $R_D(1 - T)$ as the cost of debt:

$(0.70 \times 16\%) + (0.30 \times 10\%) = 14.2\%$

Cash flow is shown in Table 5.4.

Answer 2: WACC Method

Here the required return is:

$(0.70 \times 16.5\%) + [0.30 \times 10\% \times (1 - 0.30)] = 13.3\%$

Table 5.5

Year	0	1	2	3	4
Initial outlay	(50,000)				
Revenue		20,000	20,000	20,000	20,000
Depreciation		12,500	12,500	12,500	12,500
Operating income		7,500	7,500	7,500	7,500
National tax		2,250	2,250	2,250	2,250
After-tax cash flow		17,750	17,750	17,750	17,750

This gives an NPV of:

$$-50,000 + \frac{17,750}{1.133} + \frac{17,750}{(1.133)^2} + \frac{17,750}{(1.133)^3} + \frac{17,750}{(1.133)^4} = 2,469$$

The cash flow is as shown in Table 5.5. This example illustrates a point that has been shown by Myers (1977) to be true for broad categories of projects. WACC and our recommended method (which is an adjusted present value (APV) method) give answers which are not too far apart. Since there is usually considerable uncertainty about project cash flow, a small degree of imprecision in the calculation of NPV seems acceptable.

The gain from using WACC is simplicity. NPV calculations can be done at subsidiary or division level, without any consideration in the calculations of the extra debt the project will support. The allowance for debt is made implicitly in the required return which is set centrally. A major weakness is that the method effectively assumes that all projects have equal debt capacity. If we put this unrealistic assumption aside then incremental debt must come into the calculation. If it is in the calculation then it is surely worth taking the further step of calculating tax payments realistically and allowing for interest deductability.

WACC relies on introducing two offsetting errors into the calculation: first you deduct some tax that you are not going to have to pay; then you correct the error by using an interest rate below the actual rate. The numerical errors introduced in this way may be relatively small. The damage to clear financial thinking can be much greater. Consider the following example from the US.

Borman's Complaint

Frank Borman, originally famous as an astronaut, later became chief executive of Eastern Airlines. Eastern Airlines had poor profitability and high investment allowances and paid no corporate tax. A rival airline, Delta, was more profitable and did pay tax at a marginal rate of about 50 per cent. Delta bought new planes and financed them with debt at 8 per cent. The after-tax cost of the aircraft funding was therefore only 4 per cent.

When Eastern bought planes, because it paid no tax, the after-tax cost was the same as the before-tax cost at 8 per cent. 'Unfair' cried Borman 'Why should the tax system work so that a struggling airline like mine has to pay twice as much for aircraft funding as a prosperous line like Delta? Change the tax laws and make them fairer'.

It is a test for the reader to see how quickly he can see through this argument. The playing field is level for Delta and Eastern. Neither is paying tax on the part of their revenue that goes in interest to finance their planes. The notional 4 per cent funding for Delta applies to notional after-tax cash flows. The reality is that Delta, just like Eastern, is paying 8 per cent out of pre-tax cash flows.

This example shows the confusion that can be created by thinking in terms of 'the after-tax cost of debt'. WACC has been a widely used

approach to capital budgeting. It is not wrong, but it does involve simplification and short cuts on a large scale. The right balance between simplicity
and accuracy is one for users to choose for themselves. With the availability
of good spreadsheet packages and with the greater care now given to tax
analysis and project appraisal generally, the WACC method looks in-
creasingly outdated. This is particularly true when projects are large enough
to make a fuller analysis worthwhile.

Appendix II: Another CAPM-Based Approach: Project βs

This section is based on work by Franks and Broyles (FB) although some
changes have been made. This approach goes further than the recommended
method in trying to calculate a 'project β'.

This 'project β' is then put into the CAPM formula to produce a required
rate of return for the project. Using this approach, the required return does
not depend on the amount of debt associated with the project, and the
required return is not a weighted average of the costs of debt and equity.
Debt is merely a special type of equity with a β of zero. The FB approach
calculates a project β and this sets the average cost of funds for the project
whatever mix of debt and equity is actually used. Cash flow is measured
after deduction of actual tax (i.e. allowing for interest deductibility) so
knowledge of the project's debt capacity is required for the NPV calculation.
In several respects, then, the FB method is similar to the one recommended
earlier.

There are three elements in the calculation of a project β:

(1) Ungeared industry β   Like the recommended method, the FB approach
would start with the β for the industry in which the project will operate. To
get a cost of capital for the industry rather than a cost of equity the β must
be ungeared. The formula for the 'ungeared β' (β^*) is:

$$\beta^* = \frac{\beta}{1 + D(1 - T)}$$

where T is the effective extra tax rate on equity compared to debt derived
in Chapter 4 and D is average ratio of debt to equity for the industry. β^*
could be used to calculate an average required rate of return for all projects
in the industry although the formula is slightly different from the recommended approach. We wish to be more specific and to calculate a
required rate for individual projects based on their own risk characteristics.
These characteristics are measured by two further factors.

(2) Revenue sensitivity (S_R)   This is defined as the sensitivity of project
revenue to changes in overall industry revenue. It is measured by an
elasticity type of formula:

$$S_R = \frac{\text{\% change in project revenue}}{\text{\% change in industry revenue}}$$

$S_R = 0.5$ would mean that revenues from the project would only fall by 5 per cent if the revenues of the industry as a whole fell by 10 per cent. It would also mean that project revenues would only rise half as much as the industry's if business boomed. The project may have risk that is independent of the ups and downs of the industry, but it is assumed that this risk can be diversified away and so does not affect the required rate of return.

(3) Relative operational gearing   The benefits of the project are its net cash flows and not its revenues. The sensitivity of net cash flow to revenue is called operational gearing. In a simple case, total costs are fixed costs (F) plus variable cost per unit times output $(V \times Q)$. Revenue (R) is price times quantity $(P \times Q)$.

$$\text{Net Cash Flow } C = P.Q - V.Q - F$$
$$= Q(P - V) - F$$

$$\text{Operational Gearing} = G = \frac{\text{\% change in net cash flow}}{\text{\% change in revenue}}$$

$$= \frac{dC}{C} \cdot \frac{R}{dR} = \frac{dC}{dR} \cdot \frac{R}{C}$$

Notice that $\dfrac{dc}{dR} = \dfrac{dC}{dQ} \cdot \dfrac{dQ}{dR}$

$$\frac{dR}{dQ} = P, \text{ so } \frac{dQ}{dR} = \frac{1}{P}$$

$$\frac{dC}{dQ} = -V$$

Hence $\dfrac{dC}{dR} = \dfrac{P - V}{P}$

and Operational Gearing $= G = \dfrac{dC}{dR} \cdot \dfrac{R}{C} = \dfrac{P - V}{P} \cdot \dfrac{P.Q}{C}$

$$= \frac{C + F}{C}$$

This argument assumes that C and F are the same for each year of the project's life. Franks and Broyles have, however, shown that, if they fluctuate, the present value of the net cash flow for the project can be substituted for C and the present value of annual fixed costs for F. It is necessary to calculate operational gearing for the project (G_p) and the industry (G_I). Relative operational gearing is the ratio of these two, G_p/G_I.

The overall formula for project β using the Franks and Broyles model is:

Project β = Ungeared Industry β × Project Revenue Sensitivity

$$\times \quad \frac{\text{Project Operational Gearing}}{\text{Industry Operational Gearing}}$$

$$= \quad \beta^* \times S_R \times \frac{G_P}{G_I}$$

An Example

Mylor plc is a tobacco company that is considering selling unbranded 'generic' cigarettes to large retail chains. The Project Revenue Sensitivity is less than one, because consumers are likely to switch to generics in times of economic depression and to move away from them in prosperity. Because generics are by definition unbranded, this project launch, unlike others, would not be burdened by large fixed marketing costs. The following basic information is required:

(1) Industry β	0.8
(2) Tax advantage to debt	0.27
(3) The debt-to-equity ratio in the tobacco industry	0.25
(4) Project Revenue Sensitivity	0.7
(5) Industry annual cash flow	£1.8 billion
(6) Industry annual fixed costs	£1.4 billion
(7) Project annual fixed costs	£5.0 million
(8) Project annual fixed costs	£0.7 million

From these numbers we derive:

$$\text{Adjusted } \beta \;=\; \beta^* \;=\; \frac{\beta}{(1 + D(1 - T)}$$

$$= \quad \frac{0.8}{1 + (0.25 \times (1 - 0.27))} \;=\; 0.68$$

$$\text{Project Revenue Sensitivity} \;=\; S_R \;=\; 0.7$$

$$\text{Project Operational Gearing} \;=\; G_P \;=\; \frac{5.0 + 0.7}{5.0} \;=\; 1.14$$

$$\text{Industry Operational Gearing} \;=\; G_I \;=\; \frac{1.8 + 0.4}{1.8} \;=\; 1.22$$

Hence:

$$Project\ \beta\ =\ \beta^* \times S_R \times \frac{G_P}{G_I}$$

$$=\ 0.68 \times 0.7 \times \frac{1.14}{1.22}\ =\ 0.44$$

The required cost of capital is then calculated according to the standard CAPM formula:

$$Required\ return\ =\ R_f + B\ [R_m - R_f]$$

If $R_f = 9\%$ and $\bar{R}_m - R_f = 9\%$
for the generic cigarette project the required return is:

$$9\% + 0.44\ [9\%]\ =\ 13.0\%$$

The weaknesses of the FB method are the omission of any company size effect and its requirement of a larger information input to calculate revenue sensitivity and operational gearing. For companies that are prepared to provide this information input and wish to go further than the recommended method in applying CAPM theory to their capital budgeting, the Franks–Broyles method is a good way to proceed. It does not go all the way however. The Risk Adjusted Net Present Value (RANPV) approach provided by Bierman and Smidt (1984) is more comprehensive. Unfortunately, it requires that project cash flows be specified separately for every possible pattern of stock market returns. This means that the RANPV method is not widely used in practice and it is not explained in detail here.

Study Questions

1. Strathyre plc paid a dividend of 2.5p per share nine years ago and is expected to pay 13.5p per share next year. There have been no capital issues over the intervening period. The current share price is 170p. If the company's historic growth rate is expected to continue in the future, what is Strathyre's cost of equity capital?

2. Jardine's plc is a restaurant chain which is spreading rapidly throughout the UK. The dividend next year is expected to be 4.0p per share. It is believed that the dividend can grow from that level at 20 per cent per annum for each of the four subsequent years but that the chain will then be represented in most suitable cities and the growth rate will slow to 6 per cent per year which can be sustained indefinitely. The current market price of Jardine's shares is 70p. What is Jardine's cost of equity capital?

3. A Brewing company has a β of 0.92. The risk free interest rate is 11.5 per cent. According to the Capital Asset Pricing Model (CAPM), what is the cost of equity capital of this company?

4. Morley plc is an oil company with a market capitalisation of £250 million. It is considering upgrading one of its plants so that energy costs of processing can be reduced and the proportion of lighter products in its output increased. Using the information about the oil industry in the text, recommend an appropriate required rate of return for this project. The current risk-free interest rate is 8 per cent.

5. Ptarmigan plc is a property company in North-East England with a market capitalisation of £15 million. It is considering extending its operations into Cumbria. Using the information about the property industry in the text, recommend an appropriate required rate of return for the project. (The current risk-free rate is 12 per cent.)

6. Mortonhall plc uses a financial mix of 60 per cent equity and 40 per cent debt for its business. Its cost of borrowing is 10.5 per cent and its cost of equity has been calculated to be 19.0 per cent. Mortonhall pays corporation tax at a rate of 35 per cent. Using the WACC method, what is the cost of capital for Mortonhall?

7. Goldmane plc is a magazine publisher which is considering introducing an international edition of one of its titles. Goldmane believes that sales of this type of magazine are particularly sensitive to the performance of the economy, and revenue from the project would be twice as volatile in its response to favourable or unfavourable developments in the business environment as the general revenue of the industry.

Because most of the editorial content is already being produced for the domestic edition, the fixed costs associated with the new venture will be low. They will only be 30 per cent as large as the project's expected net cash flow. For a typical investment in the industry, fixed costs are much higher and this figure is typically about 90 per cent.

Using the Franks–Broyles method and the information about the printing and publishing industry in the text, calculate the required rate of return for this project.

References and Further Reading

Allen, D., Day, R., Hirst, I. and Kwiatkowski, J. (1986) 'Equity, gilts, treasury bills and inflation', *The Investment Analyst*, October, No. 83, pp. 11–18.

Arditti, F.D. (1973) 'The weighted average cost of capital: some questions on its definition, interpretation and use, *Journal of Finance*, September, Vol. 28, No. 4, pp. 1001–7.

Bierman, H. and Smidt, S. (1984) *The Capital Budgeting Decision*, 6th edn, MacMillan.

Dimson, E. and Brealey, R.A. (1978) 'The risk premium on UK equities', *The Investment Analyst*, December, No. 52, pp. 14–18.

Dimson, E. and Marsh, P. (1984) *The Impact of the Small Firm Effect on Event Studies and the Performance of Published UK Stock Recommendations*, London Business School.

Franks, J.R. and Broyles, J.E. (1979) *Modern Managerial Finance*, Wiley.

Ibbotson, R. and Sinquefield, R. (1976) 'Stocks, bonds, bills and inflation: year by year historical returns (1926–1974)', *Journal of Business*, Vol. 49, No. 1, pp. 11–47.

Myers, S.C. (1974) 'Interactions of corporate financing and investment decisions — implications for capital budgeting', *Journal of Finance*, March, Vol. 29, No. 1, pp. 1–26.

Myers, S.C. and Turnbull, S.M. (1977) 'Capital budgeting and the capital asset pricing model: good news and bad news', *Journal of Finance*, May, Vol. 32, No. 2, pp. 321–33.

Rayner, A.C. and Little, I.M.D. (1966) *Higgledy Piggledy Growth Again*, Oxford.

Risk Measurement Service Quarterly, London Business School.

Sharpe, W.F. (1964) 'Capital asset prices: a theory of market equilibrium under conditions of risk, *Journal of Finance*, September, Vol. 19, No. 3, pp. 425–42.

6
Special Situations

Leasing

Leasing is a method by which a company can acquire the use of an asset without buying it outright. Instead, the asset is owned by a lessor organisation and the user, the lessee, pays a fixed charge every month (or other period). Lease agreements may be drawn up in a variety of different ways. Clauses may cover options to cancel the lease, service and maintenance to be provided by the lessor, and the rights to the equipment at the end of the lease period. Our discussion will concentrate on what is called a financial lease. Here the lessor is, typically, a subsidiary of a bank and the lease is drawn up so that the bank is exposed to the minimum risk. This means that:

(a) The lessee is committed to paying lease payments equivalent in value to the full cash price of the asset.
(b) The lease is non-cancellable.
(c) The lessor provides no service, maintenance or guarantee for the leased asset.

The fate of the asset at the end of the lease period varies. A common arrangement is that the lessee may opt to continue using the asset for a further period (known as the secondary lease period) in exchange for a nominal annual payment. We shall assume this method in our example. Alternatively, the residual value may go to the lessor who sells the asset, either to the lessee or elsewhere, at the end of the lease period. This can create a problem of negotiating a fair price if the lessee wants to keep the asset. Normally, the lessor must be the beneficiary of the residual value if the lease is to receive favourable tax treatment.

It is apparent from this list that the commitment to pay off a financial lease is very similar to a commitment to pay off a loan if the asset had been financed through company borrowing. Despite this similarity, accountants have historically treated them quite differently. With buy-and-borrow, both the asset and the associated debt appear on the balance sheet. A lease, however, was off balance sheet finance and neither asset nor liability would appear. Accountants have now realised the error of their ways, and in future under SSAP21 leased assets will generally be treated as owned assets and the capitalised value of lease payments as debt, where the substance of the lease agreement warrants this interpretation.

There are, however, important legal and tax differences between leasing and buying an asset. The payments made by the lessee company are a business cost and fully tax-deductible. If the company were repaying a loan, only the interest component would be deductible. Because the lessor bank is technically the owner of the asset, the bank has the right to the writing-down allowances. One motive for leasing can be tax efficiency. If the lessee is not expecting to pay mainstream corporation tax, it cannot get full value from the writing-down allowances associated with new equipment. By leasing, the allowances are effectively transferred to the bank which can use them. The bank will be forced by competition to take account of these allowances when it calculates the lease payments thus giving the lessee more favourable terms.

The decision to lease or to buy has cash flow consequences spread over a number of years. It is therefore possible to appraise leases within the same general framework using incremental after-tax cash flow which is used for investment projects. There are also important differences that affect the appraisal methods:

(1) A leasing decision is a financial decision. For projects, we have gone as far as possible to evaluate the project itself and have measured cash flows to and from the pool of debt and equity which constitutes the company's financial resources. For lease evaluation this makes no sense. We have to evaluate cash flows from the equity pool only if we want to differentiate between financing alternatives. In terms of the cash flow diagram in Chapter 2 (reproduced in Figure 6.1), lease decisions are evaluated by measuring cash flows to equity holders on a pre-personal tax basis.

(2) Lease payments, like loan repayments, are a fixed, contractual commitment by the company. They are as risk-free as possible in a commercial environment and the appropriate discount rate is therefore the risk-free interest rate. The fact that we are measuring cash flows to and from an equity pool, but are using a discount rate appropriate to debt, may seem paradoxical. In fact we are being consistent in discounting cash flows at a rate appropriate to their risk.

(3) The decision whether to lease or buy/borrow will depend only on the incremental cash flows affected by this decision. If the general decision

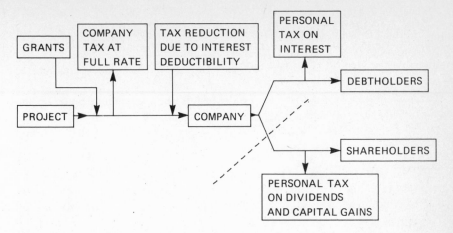

Figure 6.1   Cash Flow Boundary for Lease Evaluation

to proceed with a project has already been made, the project cash flows can be ignored in the subsequent analysis because they will be received whichever financing alternative is chosen.

(4) A lease can only be evaluated by comparison with a specific financing alternative. Because lease obligations are so similar to debt obligations, we shall normally assume that the lease takes the place of an equivalent debt, i.e. that there is 100 per cent 'debt displacement'. An analysis which compared lease financing with a debt/equity mixture would be in danger of confusing the project financing decision with the company gearing decision. In some cases, however, firms may have reached their debt limit and find that their bankers are prepared to offer a lease but are not prepared to offer a similar amount in debt. Here the proper comparison must be to acknowledge that alternative finance would have to include equity. The calculations that follow will also show how to do the sums when debt displacement is less than 100 per cent.

Because a lease is a financing method the most obvious question is, 'how much does it cost?' This suggests that we should work out the *equivalent interest rate* that is implied by the offer of a lease and compare this with the company's cost of borrowing. We want to make the comparison on an after-tax basis. This involves recognising the tax shield generated by the lease payments and the alternative tax shield generated by the writing-down allowances and the interest deductibility if the asset is bought using debt. If the company's borrowing rate is R, the after-tax cost of debt to the shareholders is $R(1 - T)$ where T is the effective company tax rate if tax relief is obtained immediately. If there is a delay of one year the after-tax cost of debt is $R[1 - T/1 + R]$. This is the rate with which the after-tax cost of leasing should be compared. The after-tax cost of leasing is simply the internal rate of return on the cash flows from the lease:

including the tax saving from the deductibility of lease payments;

including the tax loss because, as a lessee, the firm does not get the writing-down allowance;

not including the tax loss because the firm is not making interest payments on debt. The tax deductibility of debt interest is already being allowed for by setting $R(1 - T)$ or $R(1 - T/1 + R)$ as the cost of debt funding which the lease has to beat.

If this IRR is below $R(1 - T)$ or $R(1 - (T/1 + R))$, the lease is an attractive financial option. Because after-tax costs are potentially confusing, it is recommended to convert the IRR into an *equivalent interest rate* by multiplying by:

$$\frac{1}{1 - T} \quad \text{or} \quad \frac{1}{1 - \dfrac{T}{1 + R}}$$

This number is directly comparable to the interest rate quoted by the bank, and shows whether a lease offers good value.

An Example

A printing company has an opportunity to buy a new press by outright purchase or by lease. The cash price is £150,000. The alternative is a lease involving six annual payments of £33,500. The first payment would be made immediately and the last five years hence. Following this there would be a secondary lease period of a further five years during which the firm could keep the equipment for a nominal sum. It is confidently expected that the equipment would be scrapped within this period. The firm has a borrowing rate of 12 per cent and pays an effective rate of corporation tax of 28 per cent. The writing-down allowances on this type of equipment are 25 per cent of the declining balance each year. Should the lease be accepted?

Answer

The incremental cash flow from the lease is shown in Table 6.1. In this example, the lost writing-down allowances have been truncated using the method described earlier. Notice that under the pooling system the incremental WDAs will continue even if the press is scrapped (for zero residual value) before year ten. The IRR of the incremental after-tax cash flow is 9.86

Table 6.1

Year		1	2	3	4	5	6	7	8	9	10
Cash price	150,000										
Lease payments	33,500	33,500	33,500	33,500	33,500	33,500					
Tax saving on lease		9,380	9,380	9,380	9,380	9,380	9,380				
Writing-down allowance	37,500	28,125	21,094	15,820	11,865	8,899	6,674	5,006	3,754	8,447	
Tax for loss from foregone WDAs	10,500	7,875	5,906	4,430	3,322	2,492	1,869	1,402	1,051	2,365	
Incremental after-tax cash flow	116,500	(34,620)	(31,995)	(30,026)	(28,550)	(27,442)	6,888	(1,869)	(1,402)	(1,051)	(2,365)

per cent. The interest rate equivalent of this, given a one-year lag in tax payments, is:

$$\frac{9.86}{1 - \dfrac{0.28}{1.12}} = 13.15 \text{ per cent}$$

The lease is therefore more expensive than borrowing from the bank at 12 per cent and should be rejected.

Partial Debt Replacement

Suppose that, for the press example we have just considered, the correct comparison were between lease finance and a mixture of 60 per cent debt/40 per cent equity. How would the calculation be affected?

Remember first that the cash flows in this example are (virtually) risk-free, and so the cost of equity capital for this purpose is the risk-free rate of 12 per cent. The difference, of course, is that equity pays corporation tax and debt does not. A 60/40 mixture of debt and equity will have only 60 per cent of tax benefit which would be achieved by pure debt. We therefore substitute $0.60T$ for T in the last part of the calculation.

The effective cost of the lease for comparison with a 60/40 debt/equity mixture is therefore:

$$\frac{9.86}{1 - \dfrac{0.60T}{1 + R}} = \frac{9.86}{1 - \dfrac{0.60 \times 0.28}{1.12}} = 11.60\%$$

The risk-free cost of finance available in the financial marketplace (either debt or equity) is 12 per cent, so on this basis the lease is the cheaper alternative and should be accepted.

Non-Taxpaying Companies

If the printing company had not been paying tax, the calculation would have been simpler. The incremental cash flow would be calculated as shown in Table 6.2. The IRR of the cash flow is 13.47 per cent and can be compared without any further adjustment with the risk-free rate of 12 per cent. The lease is a bad buy for a non-taxpaying company whether the alternative is pure debt or a debt/equity mixture.

References and Further Reading

Franks, J.R. and Hodges, S.D. (1978) 'Valuation of financial lease contracts: a note', *Journal of Finance*, May, Vol. 33, No. 2, pp. 657–70.

Myers, S.C., Dill, D.A. and Bavista, A.J. (1976) 'Valuation of financial lease contracts', *Journal of Finance*, June, Vol. 31, No. 3, pp. 799–819.

7

Asset Life, Asset Replacement and Project Timing

There has been an important hidden assumption in our arguments so far: we have equated projects with assets. The investment decision is about purchasing an asset which will generate cash flow for a number of years. At the end of its economic life it will be scrapped and the project terminated. This coincidence of project life and asset life is, in real life, highly unlikely. A project is a business opportunity which will exist until changes in consumer taste, competitive action by rival firms, or other factors choke it off. An asset can last until vital parts corrode, bearings wear out, or for other physical reasons. It may be that technology changes will terminate the project and the economic life of the associated assets at the same time. However, we need an appraisal method that can cope with other possibilities. There are a number of different cases we need to consider.

Alternative Assets with Unequal Lives: Indefinite Project Life

An Example

Palermo Laundry plc is choosing between diesel and petrol powered delivery vans. The laundry expects vans of one sort or another to continue in operation and use into the indefinite future. Vans, though, have a limited life. Petrol vans cost £12,000 and are expected to last four years before being sold. At present prices, four-year-old petrol vans fetch £2,000. Diesel vans cost £18,250 and are expected to last six years. Six-year-old diesel vans sell for £3,000. A diesel van saves £500 per annum on lower fuel and maintenance costs compared to a petrol van. Palermo is not paying and does not expect to pay corporation tax. Its required rate of return for this purpose is 14 per cent. Which type of van is the best buy?

Answer

The answer is found by what is called the annualised cost method. Suppose that Palermo had been planning to rent vans. It would get quotations for the annual cost and would accept the petrol van only if the rental were £500 or more below the diesel van. Annualised cost simply works out to the notional rental equivalent of the purchase price and makes the same comparison.

In the case of the petrol van, the annualised cost (x) is such that the present value of x paid annually for four years just matches the cash price less the present value and the disposal value. It does not matter whether the annual payments are made at the beginning or end of each year so long as the treatment is consistent between the two types of van. We shall take payments at the end of each year when the van is in use and shall assume that the fuel and maintenance savings arise at this point too.

X is then found from:

$$\frac{X}{1.14} + \frac{X}{(1.14)^2} + \frac{X}{(1.14)^3} + \frac{X}{(1.14)^4} = 12,000 - \frac{2000}{(1.14)^4}$$

$$2.9137x = 10,816$$

$$x = 3,712$$

The annualised cost for the diesel van (Y) is calculated from:

$$\frac{Y}{1.14} + \frac{Y}{(1.14)^2} + \frac{Y}{(1.14)^3} + \frac{Y}{(1.14)^4} + \frac{Y}{(1.14)^5} + \frac{Y}{(1.14)^6}$$

$$= 18,250 - \frac{3000}{(1.14)^6}$$

$$3.8887y = 16,883$$

$$y = 4,342$$

In this case the petrol van is the winner. If the £500 extra running costs are added to its annual cost it is still cheaper than the diesel van.

Suppose that we faced the same problem against a background of 6 per cent annual inflation affecting van prices, fuel costs and maintenance alike. In this case, the annualised cost is calculated as an amount that rises with inflation, so that the payment in the second year is 1.06 times the payment in the first and so on. On this basis the annualised cost of the petrol van (Z) in current money is:

$$\frac{Z(1.06)}{1.14} + \frac{Z(1.06)^2}{(1.14)^2} + \frac{Z(1.06)^3}{(1.14)^3} + \frac{Z(1.06)^4}{(1.14)^4} = 12,000 - \frac{2000\,(1.06)^4}{(1.14)^4}$$

$$3.346\,Z = 10,505$$

$$Z = 3,140$$

It can be seen that Z could also have been calculated by doing the original calculation at the real rate of discount: $(1.14/1.06) - 1 = 7.55\%$.

On the same basis the annualised real cost for the diesel van is £3,480 and, after allowing for fuel and maintenance savings, this is cheaper than the petrol van. Making allowance for inflation (and recognising that required returns on a real basis are less than on a nominal basis) works to the particular advantage of long-lived projects. In this example it has been enough to turn the tables in favour of the diesel vans.

An alternative approach to this type of problem is the Lowest Common Multiple (LCM) method. The LCM of the life of the petrol van (four years) and the diesel van (six years) is 12 years. It is possible, therefore, to compare the costs of running a sequence of three petrol vans each lasting four years with a sequence of two diesel vans lasting six. The present values of all cash items (purchase price, scrap value, running costs) over the next 12 years are compared.

This is a perfectly good method. It will always give the same answer as the annualised cost method. The disadvantages of the LCM method are that it is more cumbersome and, because the LCM may turn out to be a large number, it appears to be making assumptions about the price and performance of petrol and diesel vans far into the future.

Assets with Variable Lives: Indefinite Project Life

In the laundry van example we have assumed that the four-year life of petrol vans is given. In fact, the question of how long to keep a van is something that the business has to decide. The technique, though, is still annualised cost. Just as the four-year-old petrol van had to compete against a six-year-old diesel van, it also has to compete against a three-year-old petrol van and a five-year-old petrol van before we can decide that four years is the optimal van life.

Consider Table 7.1. For simplicity we are assuming no inflation. The new price of the van is £12,000. We treat running costs as arising at the end of the year. In the earlier example we could ignore running costs because,

Table 7.1

Year of operation	Running costs (£)	Disposal value at year end (£)
1	3,500	9,000
2	4,500	6,000
3	5,500	3,500
4	6,500	2,000
5	7,500	1,000
6	9,000	500

except for the £500 diesel saving, they were not incremental. Here we must consider them, so annualised cost is being calculated on a different basis.

The annualised cost on the basis of a three-year life (A_3) is calculated as the annual amount, paid at the end of each year, which will just cover the purchase and running costs less the disposal value of the van:

$$\frac{A_3}{1.14} + \frac{A_3}{(1.14)^2} + \frac{A_3}{(1.14)^3}$$

$$= \ 12,000 + \frac{3,500}{1.14} + \frac{4,500}{(1.14)^2} + \frac{5,500}{(1.14)^3} - \frac{3,500}{(1.14)^3}$$

$$2.322\,A_3 \ = \ 19,883$$

$$A_3 \ = \ 8,563$$

For a four-year life the annual cost (A_4) is £8,548, and for a five-year life A_5 is £8,584. This confirms that it is best to keep the vans for four years before replacing them.

Optimal Asset Life with Changing Technology

Changing technology has a double effect on replacement decisions. On the one hand, the availability of cheaper and/or more effective equipment will encourage scrapping of old machinery. On the other hand, rapid technological improvement will give businesses a reason to hold on to old machinery because they can get even better value by replacing next year than they can now. If it can be assumed that technology is moving ahead at a steady and predictable rate, this kind of replacement decision can quite easily be analysed mathematically.

An Example

Progress in computer technology means that the cost of a computer of given capability falls by 15 per cent per year. The annual maintenance cost for a computer is 20 per cent of the initial purchase price and is paid at the end of the year in which service has been received. The computer capacity that the company needs costs £100,000 at present. If the appropriate cost of finance is 10 per cent, how long should a computer be kept in service before it is replaced? Again, for simplicity, we leave tax out of the example.

Answer

The key here is to notice that computers are effectively subject to 15 per cent 'negative inflation' and the method of working out annualised cost in an inflationary environment used in the laundry van example can be used here.

We shall treat the life of the computer as a variable, and for different lives will work out an annualised cost (B_n) which falls by 15 per cent per annum. When the computer is replaced with a new one, its price and all costs associated with it will be less than those of the first machine by the 'negative inflation' factor of 15 per cent per annum. The second machine can therefore be paid for by continuing payments on the same pattern as before, each payment smaller than the last by a factor of $(1-0.15)$. The third machine and all subsequent machines fall into the same pattern. Clearly the life-span that is optimal for the first machine will be optimal for later machines too.

Annualised costs worked out in this way are directly comparable. We choose the life-span with the lowest annualised cost in the first year, knowing that this payment, falling by 15 per cent each year, will be sufficient to maintain the company's computer capacity indefinitely.

If we keep the first computer for four years, the annualised cost B_4 (paid at the end of each year of service) is calculated as follows:

$$\frac{B_4}{1.10} + \frac{B_4(1 - 0.15)}{(1.10)^2} + \frac{B_4(1 - 0.15)^2}{(1.10)^3} + \frac{B_4(1 - 0.15)^3}{(1.10)^4}$$

$$= 100,000 + \frac{20,000}{1.10} + \frac{20,000}{(1.10)^2} + \frac{20,000}{(1.10)^3} + \frac{20,000}{(1.10)^4}$$

$$2.5739\, B_4 = 163,397$$

$$B_4 = 63,482$$

This tells us that the company could provide itself with computer capacity, replacing machines on a four-year cycle, if it paid £63,482 at the end of the first year, £53,960 (i.e. 63,482 × 0.85) at the end of the second, £45,866 (i.e. 63,482 × 0.85^2) at the end of the third, and so on.

Calculation of annualised costs on this basis for different lives gives the results shown in Table 7.2 which indicate that computers should be replaced every seven years.

Table 7.2

Computer replacement cycle (years)	Annualised cost (£)
4	63,482
5	60,668
6	59,427
7	59,057
8	59,200
9	59,654

Timing the Introduction of New Equipment

A firm may see the introduction of new equipment and techniques to its production process as inevitable, but may still have a problem deciding when to make the change. The introduction of computer controlled machine tools would be an example. These machines are a labour saving development, and as labour becomes more expensive and computer technology becomes cheaper it may be clear that the new technology will eventually be preferred. The problem is to recognise the right moment at which to switch.

An Example

A particular type of computer controlled lathe currently costs £47,000 and the price is expected to remain constant. The new lathe would replace an existing non-computerised lathe (current disposal value £14,000, disposal value declining at £1,000 per annum). The new lathe would last 10 years and would have a disposal value at the end of that period of £6,000. The new machine would make a saving of labour and associated costs of £5,000 in the current year, rising by 9 per cent per annum. The company pays no mainstream corporation tax and has a required return for this project of 15 per cent. When should the new lathe be introduced?

Answer

There are two pitfalls to avoid in this problem. One mistake is to look for the point in time where the NPV from the new machine first becomes non-negative. If the firm buys the new equipment at that time, then it is not going to get any financial benefit from the new technology for 10 years. The other mistake is to delay the new equipment until the NPV from its introduction reaches a maximum. That way the firm might miss out on a whole 10-year period during which the new technology could have been making money for it, just because the next machine would make even more.

The solution to this class of problem comes from the *first-year rule*. The firm should introduce the equipment in the first year in which the annualised incremental cost of the new machinery falls below the annual savings. The logic of this approach is clear: if the firm intends to rent the equipment, it is obvious that the new equipment should be installed if and when the annual savings exceed the incremental rental costs.

In the example, the annualised cost (X) is the annual sum, paid at the end of each year for 10 years, which is equivalent to the current purchase price less the present value of the future disposal value. We therefore solve the following equation:

$$47,000 - \frac{6,000}{(1.15)^{10}} = \frac{X}{1.15} + \frac{X}{(1.15)^2} + \cdots + \frac{X}{(1.15)^{10}}$$

$$= 5.019\,X$$

$$X = 9069$$

We want the annual *incremental* cost, so we subtract from this the annual cost of keeping the old machine. This will not be an equal amount each year. The amount that would have to be paid at the end of the current year (Y_0) to compensate for holding on to the old lathe one more year is calculated from:

$$14,000 = \frac{Y_0 + 13,000}{1.15}$$

$$Y_0 = 3,100$$

Because the disposal value falls by £1,000 per annum, Y_1 is calculated from:

$$13,000 = \frac{Y_1 + 12,000}{1.15}$$

$$Y_1 = 2,950$$

and by similar argument:

$$Y_2 = 2,800$$

$$Y_3 = 2,650$$

$$Y_4 = 2,500$$

$$Y_5 = 2,350$$

Table 7.3 shows both the costs and the benefits in annual terms. It can be seen that the new lathe should be introduced in year 3, when annual savings exceed annual incremental costs for the first time.

Table 7.3

Year	Annual cost of new lathe (£)	Annual cost of old lathe (£)	Annual incremental cost (£)	Annual savings (£)
0	9069	3,100	5,969	5,000
1	9069	2,950	6,119	5,450
2	9069	2,800	6,269	5,941
3	9069	2,650	6,419	6,475
4	9069	2,500	6,569	7,058
5	9069	2,350	6,719	7,693

It may be argued that the assumption that the price of the new lathe is constant is unduly restrictive. Suppose the cost of new technology was falling at a steady rate of 6 per cent per annum, so that the new lathe, if purchased in one year's time would cost $47,000 (1 - 0.06) = 44,180$ and the scrap value at the end of its 10-year life would be $6,000 (1 - 0.06) = 5,640$. The value of the old non-computerised lathe is not affected.

On this basis the annual cost of the new lathe can be recalculated. It will not be an equal amount each year. Remember that, in principle, the annualised cost is the amount that the firm would have to pay if it rented the equipment on a commercial basis. If prices of computer controlled lathes were falling at 6 per cent per annum, competition in the rental market would force annual rents down at this same rate. A rental organisation that buys a lathe for £47,000 today knows that in a year's time it will be in competition with other rental firms which have bought lathes for £44,180 and that it must therefore accept that rentals will decline throughout the life of a lathe.

Let the annual rental of a lathe in the current year be X_1. The rental next year will be $X_1[1 - 0.06]$ and this rate of decline will continue. We calculate X_1 from the following equation:

$$47,000 - \frac{6,000}{(1.15)^{10}} = \frac{X_1}{1.15} + \frac{X_1(1 - 0.06)}{(1.15)^2} + \frac{X_1(1 - 0.06)^2}{(1.15)^3} + \dots$$

$$+ \frac{X_1(1 - 0.06)^9}{(1.15)^{10}}$$

$$45,517 = 4.1280 X_1$$

$$X_1 = 11,026$$

The schedule of annual costs and benefits can now be modified as shown in Table 7.4.

The falling price of new lathes has changed the situation so that it is now desirable to wait until year four before introducing the new equipment. This is a specific example of the paradox that falling equipment prices can act

Table 7.4

Year	Annual cost of new lathe (£)	Annual cost of old lathe (£)	Annual incremental cost (£)	Annual savings (£)
0	11,026	3,100	7,926	5,000
1	10,365	2,950	7,415	5,450
2	9,743	2,800	6,943	5,941
3	9,158	2,650	6,508	6,475
4	8,609	2,500	6,109	7,058
5	8,092	2,350	5,742	7,693

to discourage investment because they give firms a reason to postpone action.

Replacement with More Complex Cost–Benefit Cycles

A major limitation of the first-year rule is that it assumes that the benefits of new equipment are received immediately the equipment is installed and that they rise steadily over time. The pattern may be more complex. A common example is forestry, where managers must decide when to cut down their trees and replant. The first-year rule cannot be used here: the newly planted saplings will produce very little incremental value in the first year. In some cases new manufacturing equipment may not yield its full benefits immediately because the firm will take time to learn to use it effectively.

An Example

The value of uncut timber is £1.50 per cubic foot and this price is expected to rise in line with inflation. The number of cubic feet of timber per acre depends on the maturity of the trees and rises as shown in Table 7.5. The required rate of real return is 7 per cent.

Table 7.5

Age of timber	Cubic feet per acre ('000 cu.ft)
15	5.0
16	5.7
17	6.3
18	6.8
19	7.2
20	7.5

Once again, the annualised cost approach can be used. We calculate the annual rental (measured in constant real terms) that can be paid from the proceeds of the timber when it is eventually cut. This rental will vary with the number of years the timber is allowed to grow. The best time to cut the timber is when the effective annual rental on the land reaches a maximum.

In the example, if the trees are cut after 15 years, the total proceeds (in current money) will be $5,000 \times £1.50 = £7,500$ per acre. Annual rental

Table 7.6

Years before felling	Annual rental (£)
15	298.5
16	306.6
17	306.4
18	300.0
19	288.9
20	274.4

(A_{15}) is calculated as follows (we are assuming the rental is paid at year end):

$$\frac{7,500}{(1.07)^{15}} = \frac{A_{15}}{1.07} + \frac{A_{15}}{(1.07)^2} + \cdots + \frac{A_{15}}{(1.07)^{15}}$$

$$2,718 = A_{15}(9.1079)$$

$$A_{15} = 298.5$$

Similar calculations will give the annual rental for different life-cycles of the trees (see Table 7.6).

The figures show that it is most profitable to fell the trees after 16 years. This method can also be used to compare different species of tree or, indeed, different crops that could be planted on the land. The alternative which can pay the highest rental on the land is the one to be preferred. In this simple example, the only cash flow we have considered has been the price for which the timber could eventually be sold. The present value of any cash outflows for labour and fertiliser, etc. should be subtracted from the proceeds before the annual rental is calculated.

The General Replacement Problem

We have shown that replacement problems are often best viewed on an incremental basis. The problem is not whether the new machine will be better than the old one, but whether it is best to replace it now or wait one more year.

Delaying replacement for a year involves both costs and benefits:

Costs They include the cost of maintaining, operating and feeding the old machine with raw materials for one more year. There is an added loss of salvage value because the amount will be less and there will be a delay before it is received.

Benefits All the costs of buying, operating and supplying the new machine are postponed for one more year. In addition, the cost of buying the whole chain of the new machine's eventual replacements and its running costs is also postponed for as long as the company expects to continue the business.

Looking at the problem this way makes it seem impossibly complex. Replacement decisions clearly depend on how long the underlying business will remain profitable, and how equipment prices and technology will change in the future. These things cannot be known with certainty and may move in quite unpredictable ways. In this chapter we have looked at a range of approaches to the problem which have made simplifying assumptions that make the analysis more tractable. They provide a practical and workable framework for tackling replacement decisions.

Study Questions

1. A railway company operates diesel locomotives which have a life of 15 years. It can equip them with either mild steel exhaust systems, which have a life of three years, or stainless steel systems which last five years. A mild steel system costs £500, installed, and a stainless steel one £750. Assume there will be no inflation in these prices, and the railway has a required rate of return for this type of project of 20 per cent. Which type of exhaust is the best buy? Suppose that inflation were expected to be 10 per cent per annum. Which exhaust would be preferred in this case?

2. A new car for a sales executive costs £10,000. The trade-in price of the car at the end of each year is given below as a percentage of its original price. The cost of maintenance rises every year as the car gets older, and this is also shown as a percentage of the original price.

Year	Trade-in at end of year (%)	Maintenance (paid at beginning of year) (%)
1	80	3.0
2	72	4.5
3	65	6.0
4	55	7.5
5	45	10.0
6	25	14.0

Tax can be ignored. There is no inflation. The company sets a required rate of return of 10 per cent. How long should a car be kept before it is traded in?

3. An automated supermarket checkout costs £2,100 and this price will remain constant. The equipment would have a life of seven years. There would be no scrap value. It would save 150 hours of labour per annum, labour which, in the coming year (19x2) costs £2.50 per hour. The price of labour is expected to rise at a rate of 25 pence per hour per annum. When is it worth installing the new equipment? Use 13 per cent as the required return.

4. The Commonwealth Government is considering building a railway from Alice Springs to Darwin. Construction will cost $50m and the line will become operative in the year following construction. The Operating Profit (before deducting maintenance expenditure) expected from the line in any year is as follows:

19x0	$3m
19x1	$4m
19x2	$5m

and so on, rising by $1m each year.

Annual maintenance on the line is $1m and there will be additional costs of track relaying of $5m which will be incurred 10 years after the line has been constructed, and every 10 years subsequently. If the appropriate cost of funds is 8 per cent, when should the line be constructed?

5. The management of a tropical forestry business is currently clearing part of its land and has to decide what type of tree to plant next. There are two alternatives:

Tree	Years to felling	Thousands of cubic feet per acre when felled	Price per cubic foot (£)
Softwood	15	8.5	0.85
Hardwood	25	10.5	1.75

For both types of tree, the cost of planting is £200 per acre and the cost of felling is £600 per acre. Assume there are no taxes, that prices are expected to remain constant and that the business has a required rate of return of 8 per cent per year. Which type of tree should be planted? If costs (of planting and felling) and wood prices are both rising at 3 per cent per annum, how would this affect the method of calculation?

References and Further Reading

Bierman, H. and Smidt, S. (1984) *The Capital Budgeting Decision*, 6th edn, MacMillan.
Marglin, S. (1963) *Approaches to Dynamic Investment Planning*, North Holland.

8

Risk Analysis

Sensitivity Analysis

The purpose of sensitivity analysis is to identify the specific risk factors that contribute most to the overall riskiness of the project. This information is used in one of two ways:

(i) to redesign the project so that some of the more significant risks are avoided;

(ii) to identify areas where further study could usefully be done to make more accurate forecasts of the variables.

Notice that sensitivity analysis does not directly lead to a decision to accept or reject. It simply contributes to a better decision at a later stage.

As inputs, sensitivity analysis requires identification of the key risk factors that influence a project's success. These factors will, of course, differ from project to project. Demand for the product, costs of inputs, productivity in the manufacturing process, the period time before the project dies are all examples of risk factors that might have to be considered. Each risk factor must be quantifiable, and sensitivity analysis consists of calculating the effect of changes in the factor on the NPV and IRR of the project. In these calculations, one factor is varied and the others are held at their expected values, so sensitivity analysis is applied to each factor individually rather than for the project as a whole.

To be useful, sensitivity analysis requires that something be known about the probability distribution of each risky variable. This may seem difficult information to obtain. However, any analysis of the project requires that expected values of the variables be supplied. Expected value means, roughly, a value which has a 50 per cent likelihood of turning out to be too high and a 50 per cent likelihood of turning out to be too low. Sensitivity analysis

108

requires only estimates of the same type where the probabilities are not 50 per cent. It is common to ask for '10 per cent bounds' on each variable. The 10 per cent lower bound is a number which, it is believed, has a 10 per cent chance of turning out to be too high and a 90 per cent chance to turning out too low. The 10 per cent upper bound is defined similarly for the upper end of the distribution. Five per cent bounds are sometimes preferred.

Ideally, the bounds may be determined by analysis of past data (meteorological data will assess the probability of rain on the day of the British Grand Prix, for example) or by use of established theory (an appendix shows how to use option prices to assess certain specific business risks). Often, the risk estimates will be subjective ones, that is, informed guesses. The technique is still useful, helping the decision maker to clarify the risks he feels he is running and aiding him in taking appropriate action to control them.

An Example — The Grantex Project

Grantex plc is a chemical company. It is considering the production of a new kind of foam core used in the manufacture of high-strength, low-weight composite shaped panels. These materials are mainly used in the aerospace industry. The Grantex product would be similar in performance to core materials recently introduced by two companies in the US which are being imported into the UK. The price in the US is $15.00 per pound and until technologically superior products are developed this price will remain constant. Transport costs add $4.00 to make the price in the UK $19.00 per pound. Demand in the UK is currently 270,000 pounds per annum.

Grantex has already done the development work on the new product. It would spend £13,500,000 over one year to build a plant capable of producing 1,000,000 pounds of product per annum. There will be no scrap value from this when the project ends. Direct production costs in labour and materials will be £3.70 per pound.

Grantex is confident that it will secure all the UK market if it matches the price of the imported product. Any surplus must be exported, probably to North America. In this case the effective price received by Grantex will be the American price ($15.00) less shipping charges ($4.00). Grantex requires a return of 15 per cent on a project of this type, and pays no corporation tax. The profitability of this project will be affected by four key variables:

(1) *The £/$ exchange rate* The new foam is effectively priced in dollars, but costs are in pounds. The current exchange rate is $1.55 = £1.00, and this is also the expected average rate over the project life. The lower bound for the average rate is $1.15 = £1.00 and the upper bound is $1.95 = £1.00.

(2) *The growth rate of UK consumption* This is expected to grow at 70,000 pounds per year, with a lower bound of 30,000 and an upper bound of 110,000. Growth is likely to continue steadily throughout the life of the project.

(3) *Plant operating performance* For aerospace and defence uses all products have to be tested to MOD standards. Batches that fail are sold to boatbuilders for £2.50 per pound. Grantex expects 70 per cent of output to pass, but this figure has a lower bound of 62 per cent and an upper bound of 78 per cent.

(4) *Technical obsolescence* The project will terminate abruptly when a better core material is developed. Grantex estimates that this will take seven years, with a lower bound of five years and an upper bound of nine years.

Sensitivity Analysis of the Grantex Project

The first stage is to calculate the NPV of the project based on the expected values of the risky variables. The expected values for variables are:

Operating performance (P) = 0.7
UK demand growth (G) = 70,000 lbs
Exchange rate (R) = $1.55
Project life (L) = seven years

After the cash outflow of £13,500,000 in year 0, the cash flow in each subsequent year is calculated as follows, with the calculation for year three given as an example.

	£
(1) Design output (lbs/yr)	1,000,000
(2) Operating performance	0.7
(3) Defective output (1) × [1 − (2)]	300,000
(4) UK demand for third year 140,000 + 2G	280,000
(5) UK sales — the lower of demand (4) and available output	280,000
(6) US sales (1) − (3) − (5)	420,000
(7) Dollar-linked revenue — UK sales × 19 + US sales × 11	9,940,000
(8) Dollar-linked revenue in £s (7) × 1.55	6,412,903
(9) Revenue from sale of defective output (3) × 2.50	750,000
(10) Total cash flow (8) + (9) − 370,000	3,462,903

With cash flow calculated in this way for seven years the project offers NPV = £1,583,309 and seems acceptable.

The next stage is to repeat the calculation, changing each of the risky variables in turn. First, operating performance is varied from 58 per cent to 82 per cent, while holding the other risky variables at their expected values. This produces Table 8.1. The information alone is valueless. It only becomes useful when combined with the information that the chance of an operating performance of 62 per cent or below is only 10 per cent, and the chance of a performance at or above 78 per cent is also 10 per cent. This tells us that it is quite unlikely that poor operating performance, on its own, will push the project into loss.

The information in Table 8.1 can readily be presented in graph form as shown in Figure 8.1. The NPV function is plotted, the bounds are drawn in. The triangle showing the negative NPVs for values of the variable between the two bounds is often shaded. This triangle gives a very rough picture of both the likelihood and the possible magnitude of losses. For the operating performance variable there is no triangle to shade. The project is profitable even at the lower bound.

Figures 8.2, 8.3 and 8.4 show the results of sensitivity analysis on the other three risky variables. Table 8.2 gives the values of NPV at the upper and lower bounds for each of these variables. From this analysis it is clear that the exchange rate risk and project life risk are the two greatest threats to the project. The growth rate of UK demand is a lesser, but still significant, risk and the operating performance of the plant itself is the least worrying aspect.

Once the risks have been identified, the question is what to do about them. Project life risk could be reduced if customers were prepared to sign long-term contracts, although this does not seem very realistic in the context

Table 8.1

Operating performance (%)	NPV
58	(711,633)
60	(329,142)
62	53,348
64	435,838
66	818,328
68	1,200,819
70	1,583,309
72	1,965,799
74	2,348,289
76	2,730,779
78	3,113,270
80	3,495,760
82	3,878,250

Table 8.2

		NPV
UK demand growth	30,000 lbs/yr/yr	(520,929)
	110,000 lbs/yr/yr	3,493,514
Exchange rate ($/£)	$1.15 = £1.00	11,098,629
	$1.95 = £1.00	(4,028,291)
Project life (years)	5 years	(2,227,510)
	9 years	4,906,451

of this example. Exchange rate risk is a much more suitable case for treatment. The project has, to a large extent, a dollar-linked return. The risks associated with this could be balanced if Grantex took on dollar-linked liabilities. Our analysis has, simplistically, worked with an average exchange rate during the project life rather than modelling the possible fluctuations. With this limitation, our analysis has shown that, around the $1.55 expected exchange rate, a movement of 1 per cent in the exchange rate makes a difference of about £177,000 of the Net Present Value. If Grantex borrowed $42 million (£27 million at $1.55 = £1.00), the gains and losses on its liability would roughly offset the exchange risk on the project. By making annual repayments on the load throughout the life of the project the currency risk could be roughly matched on a year-to-year basis and the danger of currency fluctuations greatly reduced.

Financial prudence usually dictates that dollar finance should be matched to dollar-based assets. Sensitivity analysis shows that in the particular circumstances of our example this rule can, and should, be bent. It indicates the right amount of dollar debt to take on if Grantex wants to minimise the currency risk interest in the project, although there will, of course, be other factors that influence Grantex's debt policy. The company should look at each of the risks involved in the project to see whether there are methods of reducing the risks without harming the average prospective returns.

The Value of Further Information

There are some risks that cannot be appraised more accurately by the expenditure of time and money: exchange rate risks would be a good example. There is very little useful analysis that a businessman can do to clarify what future exchange rates are going to be. The risk is a fact of life with which the businessman must cope as best he can. For this particular category of risk, a later section shows how the risk can be assessed in a precise and objective way at trivial cost.

Other risks fall into a different category, where the decision maker's initial appraisal of risk can be revised as a result of further investigation. Estimates

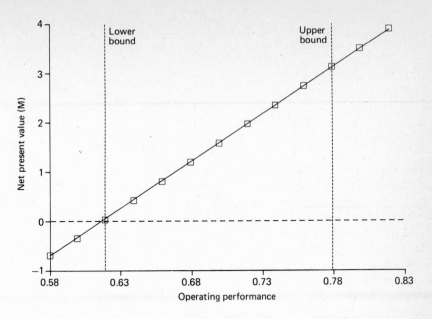

Figure 8.1   Sensitivity Analysis, Grantex Example: Operating Performance

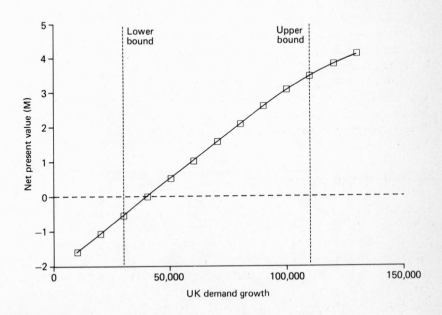

Figure 8.2   Sensitivity Analysis, Grantex Example: UK Demand Growth

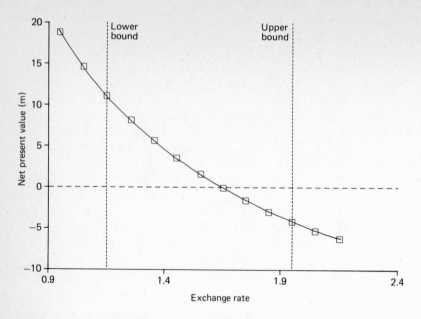

Figure 8.3   Sensitivity Analysis, Grantex Example: Exchange Rate

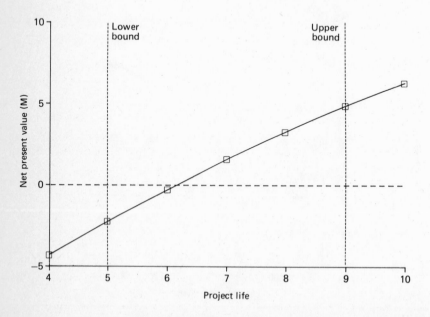

Figure 8.4   Sensitivity Analysis, Grantex Example: Project Life

of variables important to the project's success are often characterised by a point-estimate (E), usually the expected value, and a measure of dispersion (S), which may be the interquartile range, the range between the 10 per cent and 90 per cent deciles (our upper and lower bounds), or the standard deviation. The result of gathering new and relevant information will be to revise the point estimate from E to E^* and the measure of dispersion from S to S^*. In the fairly straightforward cases that we shall consider, the effect of gathering more information is to reduce risk so that $S^* < S$. The larger the sample size in a market research survey, for example, the greater the confidence that can be attached to the result. It is certainly possible, however, that in some situations research might so undermine the decision maker's original views that he ends up feeling more uncertain than when he began.

Research not only changes point estimates and dispersion estimates, it also costs money. Some of the costs are direct, but there can also be indirect costs if a good project is postponed. A project can be analysed to death. The question is, how can the benefits of further investigation be quantified so that they can be compared with the costs and so that a rational decision can be reached?

The analysis that follows involves some bold simplification, but it is a method which applies quantitative analysis to a decision that otherwise is made purely by hunch and intuition. The two main assumptions are that the probability distribution of the variable being considered is normal before and after the proposed investigation; that the distribution is described by the mean and the standard distribution; and that the amount of risk that will remain afterwards (S^*) is known. It will be convenient to illustrate the technique by returning to the Grantex example.

An Example

At present the range between the lower and upper bounds for the growth of UK demand are $110,000 - 30,000 = 80,000\,\text{lbs/yr}$. If Grantex were to commission a survey of potential customers, it believes it could reduce this range of 40,000 lbs/year. The total costs of the study, including costs of delay, would be £40,000. Is the study worth doing?

Answer

The first task is to convert the figure for upper and lower bounds into the standard deviation which is the characteristic risk measure of a normal distribution. Ten per cent bounds are 1.28 standard deviations away from the mean, and in numerical terms they are $40,000\,\text{lbs/yr}^2$ away. Hence:

$$1.28S \;=\; 40{,}000$$

$$S \;=\; 31{,}250$$

After the research has been carried out, the bounds are expected to be only $20{,}000\,\text{lbs/yr}^2$ away from the mean, so that:

$$1.28S^* \;=\; 20{,}000$$

$$S^* \;=\; 15{,}625$$

If Grantex does not do the market research study, then the uncertainty about the market will be resolved in a one-stage process by the emergence of a number with a mean of 70,000 and a standard deviation of 31,250. With the market research study, the number will emerge through a two-stage process. First, the market research will give a new point estimate (E^*) and a risk level associated with it $(S^* = 15{,}625)$ and then the true number will emerge: the same number, of course, whether the market research is carried out or not. Because the overall risk is the same, the variability associated with the new point estimate $S(E^*)$, plus the risk that remains after the market research (S^*), must equal the original risk (S). These risks are independent, and under these circumstances the variances (the squares of the standard deviations) are additive. Hence:

$$S(E^*)^2 + S^{*2} \;=\; S^2$$

$$S(E^*)^2 \;=\; (31{,}250)^2 - (15{,}625)^2$$

$$S(E^*) \;=\; 27{,}063$$

This calculation tells us what we can expect from the market research exercise. It will come up with a new point estimate (E^*) for demand growth. Before we do the research, E^* is itself an uncertain number, but its mean is 70,000 and, as we have just calculated, its standard deviation is 27,063.

We can now calculate the likelihood that the market research will cause the project to be abandoned. It follows from the sensitivity analysis that has already been carried out that NPV becomes negative if estimated demand growth goes below 39,900. This is $(70{,}000{-}39{,}900)/27{,}063 = 1.11$ standard deviations below the mean, and the probability of occurrence is 13.3 per cent. The next question is how large the average loss avoided by market research would be. In our example, there is a linear relationship between demand growth and net present value. Except in the higher ranges, where demand growth bumps up against capacity, each fall of 10,000 lbs in demand growth reduces NPV by £526,060. So the question 'Given that market research tells us whether or not to proceed, how large a loss are we likely to avoid?' can be answered by considering first: 'Given that market research tells us demand growth is likely to be below 39,900 lbs/yr^2 (1.11 standard deviation below the mean), how far below, on average, is it likely to be?' The answer depends on the truncated normal distribution, and the

Table 8.3

Cut-off point (standard deviations from mean)	Mean of observations beyond the cut-off (standard deviations from the mean)
0.0	0.80
0.2	0.93
0.4	1.07
0.6	1.21
0.8	1.37
1.0	1.52
1.2	1.69
1.4	1.85
1.6	2.02
1.8	2.20
2.0	2.36

Source: Adapted from Pearson and Lee (1909) *Biometrika*.

answer, measured in standard deviation units, can be estimated from Table 8.3. For different values of the cut-off point (in this case 1.11) the average value of observations beyond that point can be read off. By rough interpolation, the answer for our problem is 1.64. Standard deviations of 1.64 below the mean equates to a growth of $70,000 - (1.64 \times 27,063) = 25,617 \, \text{lbs}/ \text{yr}^2$ and the expected NPV associated with this demand pattern, from the earlier sensitivity analysis, is (751,500). So, if Grantex carries out the market research it has a 13.3 per cent chance that it will discover information that causes it to abandon the project, and the average loss that it avoids by doing so is £751,500. The value of the research is $0.133 \times 751,500 = £99,950$. Since the research only costs £40,000, it is worth doing.

This analysis is rough and ready. The assumption that the probability distributions are normal is, in this case, particularly important because we are looking at the tail of the distribution and it is in the tail that normal and non-normal distributions differ most greatly. The merit of the technique is that it does give some handle to a problem with considerable practical importance. Decision makers should bear in mind that they do not always have to decide to accept or reject. There is a third option, further research and investigation, that needs to be considered.

Risk Assessment and Options Markets

Risk assessments may come from many sources. They may be based on historical experience; they may be based on experienced guesswork. One opportunity to generate objective measures of risk comes from options markets. There are options markets for currencies, for interest rates, for shares, and for a range of commodities. The technique can be illustrated from the currency markets. A call option gives its owner the right to buy a specified quantity of slower commodities or currencies, at a specified price (called the exercise price or striking price) at or before an expiry date.

An Example

Rannoch plc is considering a project on 1 December 1987 whose profitability will depend on the \$/£ exchange rate on 31 March 1988. The current exchange rate is \$1.75 = £1.00. Rannoch wants to make an estimate of the likelihood that the exchange rate will take on particular values four months hence.

Answer

The point estimate is easy to get. Banks will quote forward exchange rates and for short periods into the future they are quoted in the newspapers. Forward exchange rates will differ from current exchange rates if interest rates in the two currencies differ. If dollar interest rates are lower than sterling, the dollar will be dearer in the forward market than at present. We suppose that the four-month forward rate is \$1.733 = £1.00 which corresponds to sterling interest rate 3 per cent higher than the dollar rate, which is 6 per cent. The risk associated with this estimate can be calculated from prices in the options market. The model used is the Black–Scholes option price formula. A number of assumptions underlie this model. Along with the assumption of a perfect market undisturbed by taxes or transactions costs there is also the assumption that future prices (and exchange rates) are lognormally distributed. A normal distribution with a mean of 1.733 would count it equally likely that the rate would go above 1.906 \$/£ as that it would go below 1.560 \$/£. Both numbers are 17.3 cents away from the mean. A lognormal distribution would predict that the rate is equally likely to be above 1.906 (= 1.733 × 1.1) \$/£ as it is to be below 1.575 (= 1.733 ÷ 1.1) \$/£. For small percentage changes, the difference between the two types of distribution is not very great.

The Black–Scholes formula calculates σ which is the standard deviation of the logarithm of (actual exchange rate/expected exchange rate). This logarithm is itself normally distributed, which means we can use the same normal distribution tables. The formula is:

$$O = PN(d_1) - E.e^{-rt} \cdot N(d_2)$$

where

O =   the price of a dollar option contract

P = the current exchange rate

E = the exercise price of the contract

t = the period of time the contract has to run (years)

r = the risk-free interest rate in the numeraire currency (dollars)

$\sigma\sqrt{t}$ = the standard deviation of the logarithm of

$$\frac{\text{actual exchange rate at expiry}}{\text{expected exchange rate at expiry}}$$

σ itself gives an annualised measure of risk.

$$d_1 = \frac{\ln\dfrac{P}{E} + \left(r + \dfrac{\sigma^2}{2}\right)t}{\sigma\sqrt{t}}$$

$$d_2 = d_1 - \sigma\sqrt{t}$$

$N(d_1)$ = the probability that a normal variable will take on a value below d_1 standard deviations above the mean. If d_1 is negative, the cut-off value will be below the mean and $N(d_1) < 0.50$. Values of $N(d)$ are given in Table 8.4.

$N(d_2)$ = defined as above, with d_2 taking the place of d_1

This formula can be applied to our problems as follows. Suppose that a call option with four months to run and with an exercise price of $1.70 is selling for 12.7 cents per pound. There will in fact be a range of option contracts being quoted with a range of different expiry dates and exercise prices and they would all be expected to give similar values for σ. In this case we must solve:

$$0.127 = 1.75 N(d_1) - 1.70\,(0.98)N(d_2)$$

$$\text{where } d_1 = \frac{\ln\dfrac{1.75}{1.70} + \left(0.06 + \dfrac{\sigma^2}{2}\right)0.3333}{0.5774\,\sigma}$$

$$\text{and } d_2 = d_1 - 0.5774\sigma.$$

This can be solved by trial and error or, preferably, by specialised computer packages to give:

$$\sigma = 0.20 \text{ and } \sigma\sqrt{t} = 0.1155$$

We now want to convert this information into upper and lower bounds for the exchange rate. We know that $\ln$ (actual exchange rate 31.3.88/1.733) is normally distributed with a mean zero and standard deviation of 0.1155.

Table 8.4 Area under the normal curve, $N(d)$

d	$N(d)$	d	$N(d)$	d	$N(d)$	d	$N(d)$	d	$N(d)$	d	$N(d)$
0.00	0.5000	0.50	0.6915	1.00	0.8413	1.50	0.9332	2.00	0.9773	2.50	0.9938
.01	.5040	.51	.6950	.01	.8438	.51	.9345	.01	.9778	.51	.9940
.02	.5080	.52	.6985	.02	.8461	.52	.9357	.02	.9783	.52	.9941
.03	.5120	.53	.7019	.03	.8485	.53	.9370	.03	.9788	.53	.9943
.04	.5160	.54	.7054	.04	.8508	.54	.9382	.04	.9793	.54	.9945
.05	.5199	.55	.7088	.05	.8531	.55	.9394	.05	.9798	.55	.9945
.06	.5239	.56	.7123	.06	.8554	.56	.9406	.06	.9803	.56	.9948
.07	.5279	.57	.7157	.07	.8577	.57	.9418	.07	.9808	.57	.9949
.08	.5319	.58	.7190	.08	.8599	.58	.9429	.08	.9812	.58	.9951
.09	.5359	.59	.7224	.09	.8621	.59	.9441	.09	.9817	.59	.9952
0.10	0.5398	0.60	0.7257	1.10	0.8643	1.60	0.9452	2.10	0.9821	2.60	0.9953
.11	.5438	.61	.7291	.11	.8665	.61	.9463	.11	.9826	.61	.9955
.12	.5478	.62	.7324	.12	.8686	.62	.9474	.12	.9830	.62	.9956
.13	.5517	.63	.7357	.13	.8708	.63	.9484	.13	.9834	.63	.9957
.14	.5557	.64	.7389	.14	.8729	.64	.9495	.14	.9838	.64	.9959
.15	.5596	.65	.7422	.15	.8749	.65	.9505	.15	.9842	.65	.9960
.16	.5636	.66	.7454	.16	.8770	.66	.9515	.16	.9846	.66	.9961
.17	.5675	.67	.7486	.17	.8790	.67	.9525	.17	.9850	.67	.9962
.18	.5714	.68	.7517	.18	.8810	.68	.9535	.18	.9854	.68	.9963
.19	.5753	.69	.7549	.19	.8830	.69	.9545	.19	.9857	.69	.9964
0.20	0.5793	0.70	0.7580	1.20	0.8849	1.70	0.9554	2.20	0.9861	2.70	0.9965
.21	.5832	.71	.7611	.21	.8869	.71	.9564	.21	.9865	.71	.9966
.22	.5871	.72	.7642	.22	.8888	.72	.9573	.22	.9868	.72	.9967
.23	.5910	.73	.7673	.23	.8907	.73	.9582	.23	.9871	.73	.9968
.24	.5948	.74	.7704	.24	.8925	.74	.9591	.24	.9875	.74	.9969
.25	.5987	.75	.7734	.25	.8944	.75	.9599	.25	.9878	.75	.9970
.26	.6026	.76	.7764	.26	.8962	.76	.9608	.26	.9881	.76	.9971
.27	.6064	.77	.7794	.27	.8980	.77	.9616	.27	.9884	.77	.9972
.28	.6103	.78	.7823	.28	.8997	.78	.9625	.28	.9887	.78	.9973
.29	.6141	.79	.7852	.29	.9015	.79	.9633	.29	.9890	.79	.9974
0.30	0.6179	0.80	0.7881	1.30	0.9032	1.80	0.9641	2.30	0.9893	2.80	0.9974
.31	.6217	.81	.7910	.31	.9049	.81	.9649	.31	.9896	.81	.9975
.32	.6255	.82	.7939	.32	.9066	.82	.9656	.32	.9898	.82	.9976
.33	.6293	.83	.7967	.33	.9082	.83	.9664	.33	.9901	.83	.9977
.34	.6331	.84	.7995	.34	.9099	.84	.9671	.34	.9904	.84	.9977
.35	.6368	.85	.8023	.35	.9115	.85	.9678	.35	.9906	.85	.9978
.36	.6406	.86	.8051	.36	.9131	.86	.9686	.36	.9909	.86	.9979
.37	.6443	.87	.8078	.37	.9147	.87	.9693	.37	.9911	.87	.9980
.38	.6480	.88	.8106	.38	.9162	.88	.9699	.38	.9913	.88	.9980
.39	.6517	.89	.8133	.39	.9177	.89	.9706	.39	.9916	.89	.9981
0.40	0.6554	0.90	0.8159	1.40	0.9192	1.90	0.9713	2.40	0.9918	2.90	0.9981
.41	.6591	.91	.8186	.41	.9207	.91	.9719	.41	.9920	.91	.9982
.42	.6628	.92	.8212	.42	.9222	.92	.9726	.42	.9922	.92	.9983
.43	.6664	.93	.8238	.43	.9236	.93	.9732	.43	.9925	.93	.9983
.44	.6700	.94	.8264	.44	.9251	.94	.9738	.44	.9927	.94	.9984
.45	.6736	.95	.8289	.45	.9265	.95	.9744	.45	.9929	.95	.9984
.46	.6772	.96	.8315	.46	.9279	.96	.9750	.46	.9931	.96	.9985
.47	.6808	.97	.8340	.47	.9292	.97	.9756	.47	.9932	.97	.9985
.48	.6844	.98	.8365	.48	.9306	.98	.9761	.48	.9934	.98	.9986
.49	.6879	.99	.8389	.49	.9319	.99	.9767	.49	.9936	.99	.9986

Note: For $d < 0$, use the relationship $N(d) = 1 - N(-d)$.

The 10 per cent upper bound is 1.28 standard deviations above the mean and the lower bound 1.28 standard deviations below.

For the upper bound (B_u)

$$ln\left(\frac{B_u}{1.733}\right) = 1.28 \times 0.1155$$

$$B_u = 2.01$$

and for the lower bound (B_l)

$$ln\left(\frac{B_l}{1.733}\right) = -1.28 \times 0.1155$$

$$B_l = 1.49$$

These figures suggest that the bounds for sensitivity analysis should cover a 26 cent swing either way over a four-month period. These may seem very wide bounds over a comparatively short period of time. For longer forecasts, the same estimate of σ could be used to give estimates and, of course, the bounds would widen the further ahead the forecast was being made.

There is a very human tendency for forecasters to overestimate their own abilities and to put unrealistically narrow bounds round their estimates. Where it is possible to come up with objective risk estimates as in this example it is helpful to do so. Several well-known UK companies have put themselves in financial difficulty because they have been caught out by unexpected exchange rate changes. Tools are now available to assess this risk and other financial and commodity risks, and hedging techniques to avoid their adverse impact. Companies need to know how to use them.

Monte Carlo Simulation

Unlike sensitivity analysis, Monte Carlo simulation is designed to look at the overall risk of a project as an aid to the decision to accept or reject. This requires, of course, that the variability of all the risk factors be considered together.

The inputs for simulation are the probability distributions for the individual risk factors. A fuller description of this distribution is needed than for sensitivity analysis. If the decision maker is prepared to assume that the distributions are normal, the full probability can be deduced from knowledge of the upper and lower bounds. This is the approach we shall take in our example.

The output of simulation is a probability distribution for the NPV or IRR of the project. The output is usually presented in the form of a cumulative probability diagram, so that the decision maker can read off the answers to such questions as 'What is the probability that we will lose money on this project?' or 'What return can I be 90 per cent sure we will get from the project?'

The method is simply to simulate the project on a computer a large number of times. For each simulation a value of each risk variable is drawn randomly from the appropriate probability distribution. With these figures, the NPV and IRR for the project are calculated. After several hundred simulations, a distribution of the values of NPV and IRR is drawn up.

An Example

We return to the Grantex example, and assume that all four risk variables are normally distributed. Each variable is to be simulated by a double digit random number, and a 'lookup table' is needed for each variable so that the random number can be converted into a value for the variable. We shall describe the construction of the lookup table for the proportion of output that passes quality tests.

The 10 per cent bounds are 62 per cent and 78 per cent, that is, 8 per cent either side of the mean. For a normal distribution, 10 per cent bounds are, roughly, 1.28 standard deviations from the mean and, approximating again, we shall take the standard deviation of the distribution to be 6 per cent. We shall simplify the normal distribution by considering on 13 possible discrete values for operating performance, from 58 per cent (2 standard deviations below the mean) to 82 per cent (2 standard deviations above) by intervals of 2 per cent.

Figure 8.5 shows how the bell-shaped normal curve can be divided and probabilities roughly assigned to each of the discrete values. To illustrate the method, consider the probability to be attached to an operating performance of 58 per cent. The next discrete point is 60 per cent and the halfway

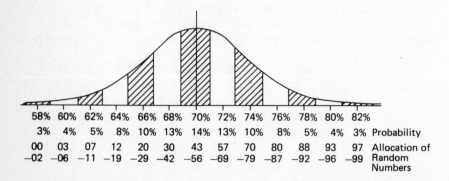

Figure 8.5 Probability Density

Table 8.5 Random Number Allocation Tables

Operating performance (%)		UK demand growth (lbs/yr²)		Exchange rate ($/£)		Project life (yrs)	
Random Nos.	Variable	Random Nos.	Variable	Random Nos.	Variable	Random Nos.	Variable
00–02	58	00–02	10,000	00–02	0.95	00–06	4
03–06	60	03–06	20,000	03–06	1.05	07–17	5
07–11	62	07–11	30,000	07–11	1.15	18–37	6
12–19	64	12–19	40,000	12–19	1.25	38–61	7
20–29	66	20–29	50,000	20–29	1.35	62–81	8
30–42	68	30–42	60,000	30–42	1.45	82–92	9
43–56	70	43–56	70,000	43–56	1.55	93–99	10
57–69	72	57–69	80,000	57–69	1.65		
70–79	74	70–79	90,000	70–79	1.75		
80–87	76	80–87	100,000	80–87	1.85		
88–92	78	88–92	110,000	88–92	1.95		
93–96	80	93–96	120,000	93–96	2.05		
97–99	82	97–99	130,000	97–99	2.15		

point between these two is 59 per cent which is, roughly, 1 5/6 = 1.83 standard deviations from the mean. From the normal distribution tables, the probability of a value more than 1.83 standard deviations below the mean is 3 per cent (measured to the nearest 1 per cent). Because we are simulating with double-digit random numbers, we cannot work in units smaller than 1 per cent.

The allocation system shown in Figure 8.5 is only one possibility. What is important is that three of the 100 numbers in the range 00 to 99 should be allocated to 58 per cent and 14 should be allocated to 70 per cent etc. Using the allocation system shown, if the random number drawn to simulate operating performance is 65, this would be converted into an operating performance of 72 per cent. An allocation system for all four variables, developed in the same way, is shown in Table 8.5.

Each simulation starts by drawing four double-digit random numbers, one for each variable. These are converted into values of the variables and NPV and IRR are calculated (see Tables 8.6 and 8.7).

For the Grantex example, this simulation was carried out 500 times. The 500 NPVs that this produced were then ranked from the lowest to the highest. The lowest was (9,437,797) followed by (8,803,481) and (8,323,536). We would interpret this as showing that there is a 100 per cent chance that

Table 8.6 Simulation 1

Variable	Random no.	Value	
Operating performance	21	66%	
UK demand growth	06	20,000	NPV = (3,238,953)
Exchange rate	59	1.65	IRR = 6.87%
Project life	38	7	

Table 8.7 Simulation 2

Variable	Random no.	Value		
Operating performance	25	66%		
UK demand growth	95	120,000	NPV	= 4,595,123
Exchange rate	44	1.55	IRR	= 23.40%
Project life	72	8		

the achieved NPV will not be lower than (9,437,797), a 99.8 per cent chance it will not be lower than (8,803,481) and a 99.6 per cent chance it will not be lower than (8,323,536). The probabilities for the 500 NPVs can be listed in this way in tabular form, but it is easier to present the results in a graph. Figure 8.6 shows, for each possible NPV, the probability that it will be reached or exceeded. Figure 8.7 shows the same information for the 500 IRRs produced by the simulations.

What is the likelihood of losing money on this project? From Figure 8.6 there is a 60 per cent chance of a positive NPV, so the chance of making a loss must be 40 per cent. What is the chance of making a 30 per cent rate of return? From Figure 8.7 there is a 20 per cent chance of making or bettering this return.

In this way Monte Carlo simulation gives the decision maker a more

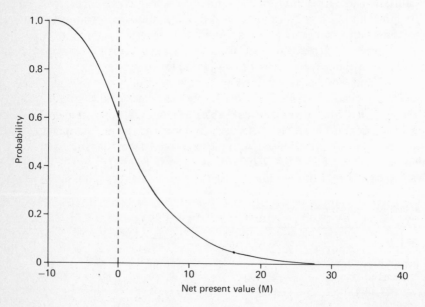

Figure 8.6 Monte Carlo Simulation, Grantex Example: Net Present Value

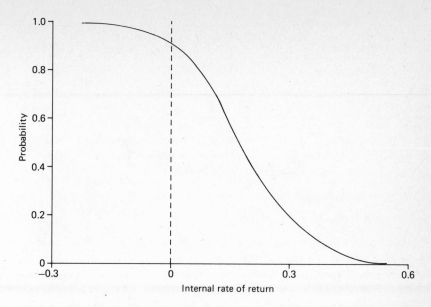

Figure 8.7   Monte Carlo Simulation, Grantex Example: Internal Rate of Return

complete picture of the risks in the project. It is then for him to decide whether he can live with them.

Simulation, despite all the mathematical manipulation involved, does not measure anything very precisely. It often builds on no more than subjective estimates of the riskiness of key variables. Nevertheless it does a useful job of putting these estimates together into a coherent picture of the risk of the project as a whole.

Notice, finally, that the extreme tails of the distribution are the most unreliable and will be sensitive to the way in which the probability distributions (in our case the normal distribution) have been approximated. The question 'How large a loss would we make in the worst 1 per cent of outcomes?' is not very accurately answered by this kind of simulation.

Inter-Related Variables

There has been an important hidden assumption in the simulation so far. It is that all the risks are entirely independent of each other. There is no reason, in general, why this should be true. Close consideration of projects will often suggest links between the risk factors.

The Grantex example is a case in point. Operating performance, the exchange rate, and the period before the project is terminated by technological progress all seem to be independent risks. But demand growth is likely to be influenced by price, and price (in pounds) will be a direct function of the exchange rate. To some extent, therefore, exchange risk and demand growth risk will offset each other. A high value for the pound will mean that Grantex gets a poor price for its product, but at least the low price in pounds should stimulate demand.

An Example

Suppose we believe that UK demand growth will be determined partly by the exchange rate and partly by other autonomous factors. Suppose we believe that the relative weight of these two items is:

60 per cent exchange rate

40 per cent autonomous factors

Technically, this implies that the exchange rate movements will account for 60 per cent of the variance of UK demand growth.

The problem, then, is to modify the simulation to take this linkage into account. Notice that the job would be easy if the exchange rate accounted for 100 per cent of the uncertainty about demand growth. In this case the two numbers would be rigidly linked and it would be necessary to draw only one random number to simulate both of them. A drawing of 83, for example, would indicate both an exchange rate of 1.85 and a growth of demand of $100,000\,\text{lbs/yr}^2$.

To cope with partial linkage we need to simulate demand growth twice: once independently (producing growth rate G_1), and once using the random number from the exchange rate (producing rate G_2). The number that we want is some sort of average of G_1 and G_2, which we shall call G^*. The averaging process will use the weights $W_1 = 0.40$ (the weight to be attached to the independent forecast) and $W_2 = 0.60$ (the weight to be attached to the exchange rate linked forecast). We need to take the average in a special way so that the overall risk of G^* is the same as the risk of G_1 and G_2. We do not want the averaging process to reduce the risk because we want the variability of demand growth to be the same in this problem as it was in the earlier case where all the risks were independent. This rules out a formula like $G^* = W_1 \cdot G_1 + W_2 \cdot G_2$.

We could get the right level of risk for G^* by setting:

$$G^* = \sqrt{W_1} \cdot G_1 + \sqrt{W_2} \cdot G_2$$

but this would give us too high an average value. We want the average value of G^* still to be 70,000 so we have to subtract a term to preserve this property. The formula that meets all our requirements is:

$$G^* = \sqrt{W_1} \cdot G_1 + \sqrt{W_2} \cdot G_2 - 70{,}000\,(\sqrt{W_1} + \sqrt{W_2} - 1)$$

Hence, if the independent simulation of growth gave 80,000 and the exchange rate simulation gave 110,000, our weighted combination of these two would be:

$$G^* = \sqrt{0.40} \cdot 80\,000 + \sqrt{0.60} \cdot 110\,000 - 70\,000\,(\sqrt{0.40} + \sqrt{0.60} - 1)$$

$$G^* = 50\,596 + 85\,206 - 28\,494$$

$$G^* = 107\,308$$

Our original simulations gave only thirteen discrete possible values for demand growth. This was simply a convenient approximation. It does not matter that the averaging process gives intermediate values. G^* as calculated here can be employed directly in the calculation of NPV and IRR.

Figure 8.8 shows the distribution of NPV modified to reflect the link between exchange rates and demand growth with the original distribution shown as an interrupted line. The difference is significant: the 10 per cent upper limit for NPV falls from £11.65 m to £9.44 m. It is important always to consider whether there are links between the risky variables when carrying out Monte Carlo simulation.

The existence of inter-related variables also points out limitations of the Monte Carlo simulation. The risk in any new project is likely to be related to risks already inherent in the firm's existing business. A project by a food manufacturer to introduce a line of ice cream would be at risk from the British weather. If the firm already made cold-weather foods such as

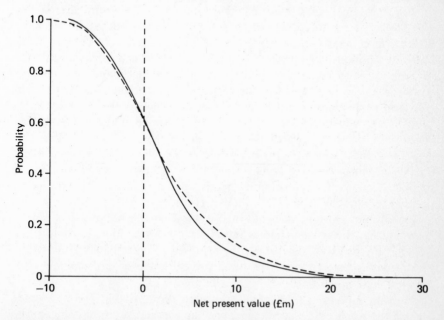

Figure 8.8 Monte Carlo Simulation, Grantex Example: Net Present Value (£m)

sausages and soup, the new project could be seen as reducing the risk in the company's overall business, even though the project on its own had considerable risks. Investments in new technologies that might grow to threaten a firm's existing business can often be justified by considering their impact on the overall risk level of the firm.

Abandonment Value

If things turn out badly for the project, is there an opportunity for the firm to cut its losses? In the Grantex example, our worst case showed the company making a loss of almost £9.5 million on an initial investment of £13.5 million. If, as we have assumed, the unfavourable prospects become clear as soon as the plant goes into production, the company may be able to change course and limit its losses to something less than £4 million.

The appropriate abandonment strategy will vary with circumstances. It might involve selling off plant and equipment which has alternative uses to another company; it might involve finding another use for them within the firm. Abandonment value might come from land and buildings that can be converted to other uses. The option to abandon will exist throughout the life of the project but it is usually a one-way option. Once a project has been abandoned it cannot be reinstated, even if prospects take a major turn for the better. In some cases, 'mothballing' a plant may offer a third alternative: if a project is reprieved, abandonment can be reconsidered in the next period. The comparison is *not* between the cash received from abandonment and the cash received from running the project to the end of its natural life. Looking at it this way biases the decision towards abandonment. The correct comparison is between the cash from abandonment and the cash received from continuing the project and reviewing the abandonment decision each subsequent period. The situation can be modelled mathematically by working backwards from the end of the project life. First, the conditions under which the project would be abandoned one year early are established, then the conditions for abandonment two years early, and so on. We do not offer an example of this kind of analysis. The reader is referred to work by Robichek and Van Horne (1967).

The Grantex example does not involve these complications, because it is assumed that the risky variables reveal themselves as soon as the project starts. If the project's assets could be disposed of immediately the adverse circumstances reveal themselves for a present value of £7.5 million, and Grantex need not absorb a loss greater than £13.5 m − £7.5 m = £6 m. This would modify the Monte Carlo simulation so that (£6 m) would become the worst possible outcome, and the cumulative probability distribution would have to be adjusted accordingly.

Appendix: The Eurotunnel

The project to establish a rail connection between Britain and France via a tunnel under the English Channel is one of the largest and most prominent single investment projects of the later 20th century. It is a project unlike those considered in our examples because the single project is the whole company. All the same, it is interesting to look at the project, taking the cash flow forecasts as given, and commenting on the appraisal methods used in the light of our earlier recommendations.

In the Preliminary Prospectus dated 26 September 1986, the IRR offered by the project is presented as follows:

Return on the project (pre-tax)	16.7%
Return on the project (post-tax)	14.1%
Project return attributable to shareholders (post-tax)	17.7%
Net dividend return (on public offering)	15.0%
Gross dividend return (on public offering)	16.6%

The prospectus also offers calculations of the sensitivity of these returns to changes in the assumptions, for example:

	Return on the project (*post-tax*)
Base case	14.1%
Assuming 20 per cent increase in operating costs throughout	13.7%
Assuming 20 per cent reduction in revenue throughout	12.2%
Assuming capital expenditure increased by 20 per cent throughout	13.0%
Assuming construction delay of one year (and extra associated cost)	13.1%

The questions which would most interest potential investors in the project are:

(a) Which measure of return is the important one?
(b) Against what standard should it be compared?
(c) How can the risk aspects of the project be incorporated into the assessment?

First, consider the appropriate measure of return. Our general recommendation has been to look at post-tax project return. A figure of 14.1 per cent will be a slight understatement of the return as we would measure it, because of the deduction of all corporate tax without allowing for reclaimable ACT.

The Channel Tunnel does not fall clearly into a defined industrial group. Contracting and Construction has an industry risk premium of 7.0 per cent, Shipping and Transport has 5.2 per cent. Let us take the lower of these figures for the moment. The project surely qualifies as a new business area, so the risk premium for this project would be at least 5.2% × 1.40 = 7.3%. It is a large project, so there is no adjustment for company size to be made. The risk-free rate in late 1986 was about 10 per cent, so the required return would be 10% + 7.3% = 17.3%. The prospective returns on the project fall considerably short of what is required.

One feature of the project is the high level of gearing associated with it. Roughly £5 billion is needed for the tunnel and of this 80 per cent is to be provided by banks and loans. There is only £1 billion of equity. This seems to suggest that the banks take a highly sanguine view of the risks of this project compared with the great majority of projects undertaken by commercial firms. Given this large amount of debt, are the returns to shareholders satisfactory?

Here it is the gross dividend return (16.6 per cent) which is the appropriate measure of return from the shareholder viewpoint. The higher figure for 'project return attributable to shareholders' is not relevant because some of these returns are neither distributed immediately to shareholders nor invested in other profitable projects. The need to hold some liquid funds in the company lowers the shareholders' return, and the return after this item is the right one to consider. If the Eurotunnel shares have simply an average level of risk, the required return of the shareholder level would be:

Risk-free rate + Risk premium on the market

= 10% + 9% = 19%

Even on this basis, the return offered is inadequate. The fact that the project itself has many of the characteristics of a new venture, and the risk at shareholder level is being substantially increased by high gearing, both suggest that an above-average risk premium would be appropriate. In short, the project simply does not measure up on the basis of the cash flow forecasts in the prospectus.

This, of course, is not the same as saying that the project itself is an unattractive investment. An investor might believe that the forecasts of traffic are unduly conservative or that the estimates of construction costs are inflated. But the shares offered in the September 1986 prospectus were apparently sold to institutions only after their arms had been twisted by the Bank of England. The later tranche of shares offered to the public in November 1987 was undersubscribed and the shares quickly went to a 33 per cent discount. These facts suggest that the appraisal in the market was not very different from our own analysis above.

Finally, consider the sensitivity analysis offered in the prospectus. We would argue that it is not much use knowing that a 20 per cent overshoot in capital expenditure will reduce the return from 14.1 per cent to 13.0 per cent, if we have no indication of how likely such an overshoot is. One chance in three, or one chance in thirty? The analysis in the prospectus is clearly incomplete and brokers' analysts and financial journalists have been left to undertake their own surveys of cost overruns on comparable projects in the past.

Study Questions

1. A large mining company is considering developing a copper mine at Mt. Ada. The total cost of establishing the mine would be £10 million. This money would be spent and the mine would become operational one year from now. The equipment would be capable of processing 200,000 tons of ore per annum and extracting 6,000 tons of copper. The annual running cost of the mine would be £4,000,000. The company has a required rate of return of 15 per cent.

   Two factors affecting profitability of the project are subject to risk. The ore body is believed to total 1 million tons, but there is a 5 per cent chance this figure may turn out to be greater than 1,200,000 tons and a 5 per cent chance that it will turn out to be less than 800,000 tons. It is expected that the copper can be sold at a price of 60p per pound but there is a 5 per cent chance that it will average below 40p. Assume that no taxes are payable and that the average price is maintained through the life of the mine (there are 2,240 lbs in a ton).

   (a) What is the NPV of this project based on the expected values of the variables?
   (b) Carry out sensitivity analysis on the two risky variables and, in the light of this, comment on proposals:
      (i) that the company should spend an additional £1 million to find out the exact amount of ore before deciding whether to invest (this would not delay the project);
      (ii) to contract to sell the whole output of the mine at a fixed price of 57p.
2. BEN Electronics is considering buying a new machine and using it to produce a new type of silicon chip that the company's engineers have designed. The financial estimates supplied by the firm's technical and marketing staff are as follows. One number is given for figures that are certain. Where there is risk, the analysts have been asked for an expected value and a feasible range of values. The probability that the final outcome will be below the lower limit, or that it will be above the high limit, is 5 per cent.

The new machine will cost £600,000 (certain), and it has a design capacity of 1 million chips a year. The proportion of these chips that will be of saleable quality is estimated at 80 per cent (range 68 per cent to 92 per cent). The fixed costs of operation will be £100,000 per annum (certain) and the variable costs will be 10p per chip (certain). Initially chips will be sold at what the market will bear. This is expected to be 50p (range 45p to 55p). However, competitors will learn to make the chips in four years (range three years to five years) and after this happens the price will fall to 30p. BEN's cost of capital for this project is 15 per cent. The machine, and the chips it produces, will become obsolete after eight years of production (no scrap value).

Perform sensitivity analysis on this project. Which type of risk (percentage of saleable chips, number of years before competitive entry and initial price) has the biggest influence on the profitability of the project? (The variable costs are only incurred on chips that are of saleable quality.)

3. Suppose that we have more details on the risk of the project in question 2. Suppose, contrary to the assumptions in question 2, that the distribution of each of the risky variables is as shown in Table A8.1. Using the Monte Carlo technique, make two simulations of the outcome of this project. Explain how a large number of simulations would help to measure the overall risk of the project. An extract from a table of random numbers is given in Table A8.2.

Table A8.1

Initial price		% of output that is saleable		Number of years before competitors enter	
Probability	Price	Probability	%	Probability	Years
0.333	45p	0.05	65	0.30	4
0.333	50p	0.10	70	0.50	5
0.333	55p	0.20	75	0.20	6
		0.30	80		
		0.20	85		
		0.10	90		
		0.05	95		

Table A8.2

81525	72295	04839	96423	24878
29676	20591	69086	26432	46901
00742	57379	39064	66432	84673

Table A8.3

Probability	Number of passengers
0.10	60,000
0.20	80,000
0.30	100,000
0.30	120,000
0.10	140,000

Table A8.4

Probability	Number of years before the bridge is complete
0.20	8 years
0.30	9 years
0.30	10 years
0.20	11 years

4. McBrawn plc is considering setting up a ferry service across the mouth of a sea loch. The initial cost of buying the boat and building the piers would be £200,000. The annual running costs would be £20,000. There are no taxes involved and McBrawn's required return for this project is 10 per cent. There are three uncertainties involved in the project. These are:

   (a) The number of passengers per annum. The probability distribution is estimated as shown in Table A8.3.
   (b) The charge per passenger. This must be approved by the local authority. Two prices seem likely. The company expects to be allowed to charge 70p but thinks that there is a 40 per cent chance that it will be able to charge only 50p.
   (c) It is planned that a bridge will eventually be built across the river. When this happens the ferry business will have to close. The piers and the boat will be worth nothing. The estimate of when the bridge will be built is shown in Table A8.4. Explain how Monte Carlo simulation could be used to analyse the risk of this project. Make two simulations (using the random numbers in question 3).

How could the simulation be done if two of the variables were inter-related? Specifically, suppose that the probability distribution for the number of passengers depended on the fare charged.

Explain how the results of Monte Carlo simulation can be displayed.

5. Consider the ferry problem in question 4, but suppose that the information about the risky variables is changed as follows:

(a) The fare is known to be 60p.

(b) The life of the bridge is known to be eight years.

(c) The estimate for the number of passengers per annum has a mean of 100,000. The 10 per cent upper bound is 140,000 and the 10 per cent lower bound is 60,000, and probability distribution is normal.

All other details of the project are as given in question 4.

Calculate the NPV of the project based on the expected value of the number of passengers.

A market research company offers to carry out a survey which could reduce the uncertainty about the number of passengers. The new estimate would reduce the distance between the 10 per cent upper bound and the 10 per cent lower bound from 80,000 to 40,000 passengers per annum. The market research company would charge £20,000 for its survey which could be carried out quickly and would not delay the project. Should the survey be commissioned?

References and Further Reading

Black, F. and Scholes, M. (1973) 'The pricing of options and corporate liabilities', *Journal of Political Economy*, May–June, Vol. 81, No. 3, pp. 637–54.

Hertz, D.B. (1964) 'Risk analysis in capital investment', *Harvard Business Review*, January–February, pp. 95–106.

Hertz, D.B. (1968) 'Investment policies that pay off', *Harvard Business Review*, January–February, pp. 96–108.

Hillier, F.S. (1969) *The Evaluation of Risky Interrelated Investments*, North Holland.

Hillier, F.S. (1971) 'A basic model for capital budgeting of risky inter-related projects', *Engineering Economist*, Fall, Vol. 17, No. 1, pp. 1–30.

Robichek, A.A. and Van Horne, J.C. (1967) 'Abandonment value in capital budgeting', *Journal of Finance*, December, Vol. 22, No. 4, pp. 577–90.

9

Conclusion: Making Project Appraisal Work

The Success of Modern Appraisal Methods

Walking down a city street at night, you come across a man who is clearly searching for something on the ground around one of the street lights. 'What have you lost?' you ask. 'My wallet' he replies, and you spend several minutes helping him look for it. 'Are you sure you dropped it here?' you ask. 'Oh no', replies the man, 'I dropped it over in the alley, but the light is so much better over here'. This is a well-known tale in business schools. The moral is that it is important to address the real problems that businesses face and not to waste time on hypothetical ones which happen to be easier or more fun to solve.

How well do the preceding chapters measure up to this test? They have covered a wide variety of techniques, some of them more sophisticated than others. It has been pointed out earlier that modern appraisal methods have been widely adopted in the business world. It is interesting to look specifically at the adoption rates for the different quantitative techniques. A recent survey by Pike and Wolfe (1987) of appraisal methods in 100 large UK

Table 9.1

Technique	Percentage of companies using it
Payback	92
IRR	75
NPV	68
Sensitivity analysis	71
Probability analysis/simulation	40
Mathematical programming	21

quoted companies showed the percentages of companies using some of the techniques covered in this book (see Table 9.1). The figures give the proportion of firms which ever use the technique. 84 per cent use either NPV or IRR which demonstrates the wide acceptance of DCF techniques. The programming methods also seem to be used infrequently and this seems to agree with the cautious view of the technique adopted earlier. Simulation is an intermediate case, but the evidence from Pike and Wolfe's survey is that those who do use the technique use it quite often and that the use of simulation is growing rapidly. In general, Pike and Wolfe's survey and other studies tend to confirm that a wide range of quantitative appraisal techniques are proving useful to large and medium-sized UK firms, and that the range of techniques being used is tending to rise.

Criticism of Modern Appraisal Methods

Modern project appraisal, however, faces three main criticisms of its performance in practice:

1. The formal calculations are only used to back up or to reinforce decisions that have effectively already been taken by senior management relying on instinct and 'feel'.

   There is evidence from surveys and anecdotes that this is a genuine problem. An extreme example is of the financial analyst who was told that the company was going to spend money redecorating the canteen and would he please do the numbers to show that it was a sound investment. In this case the error is compounded because the project is not analysable by conventional means in any case.

   This criticism highlights the gulf between stage 3 on King's categorisation of the appraisal process (evaluation) and stage 4 (decision). Evaluation is the special province of the trained financial analyst. Decision is the preserve of senior management, and those below them in the organisation are rarely allowed to forget this. It follows that the purpose of the evaluation stage is not to come up with a firm conclusion that senior managers can be asked to rubber-stamp. Senior managers will simply refuse to play that game. Instead, the objective is to provide the basis for a well-informed debate from which the decision will finally emerge.

   It is in this area that sensitivity analysis is particularly useful. Managers may easily disagree about the likely sales of a new product or the full costs to the organisation of a large computerisation project. With sensitivity analysis, each senior executive can see the outcome if his own judgement is correct and can argue with his colleagues accordingly. It may be possible to show that the project stands up even with the most pessimistic cases.

There are also likely to be unquantifiable factors. The redecoration of the canteen would have a favourable effect on the morale of the workforce. For a large consultancy fee, a psychologist might be willing to put a figure on the benefits. The project is too small to justify the cost, so management will have to proceed by 'feel'. There are much more significant benefits which may be impractical to quantify. The long-term benefits of gaining familiarity with new technology, or developing a partnership with a large company overseas, can be very significant, but difficult to quantify. In these cases the best that project appraisal can do is to quantify those aspects that can be quantified and to express them in NPV or other terms, and then to list the non-quantifiable benefits and disbenefits. It will be for the judgement of top management finally to balance the different items against each other.

There are therefore two sides to the criticism that senior managers pay more attention to their own prejudices and preconceptions than to the results of formal investment appraisal. A part of the blame certainly rests with senior management which has not learned to use modern management techniques. A part must also rest with analysts who do not produce their results in the form that is most useful to the final decision makers.

2. The second criticism is that all the projects that are put forward for analysis are made to look good, so formal analytical techniques can do little to choose between them. This criticism is particularly prevalent in large companies with a set of forms that must be filled in for any capital appropriation. They may include instructions for working out the IRR or NPV. If it is company policy to require a 20 per cent return, then all the projects will offer projections that meet the target.

There are solutions to this problem. The first is rather trivial: some companies keep their required rates of return secret to avoid bias. It is doubtful how successful this is. Rumours about the rate are likely to circulate, and the instinct of proposers to make their projects look good is not likely to be diminished.

The best answer is post-acceptance analysis, the last of King's six stages. There are two main benefits from this procedure:

(a) Future estimates can be made more realistic. It may become apparent that the costs of putting new production facilities are being consistently underestimated. The errors may be 'honest' ones or may come from the sponsors of these projects putting bias into the figures to give their projects a better chance of acceptance. In either case, it is important that forecasts be checked against subsequent events.

(b) Corrective action can be taken for current projects. In an extreme case, the project may need to be abandoned because the results fall so far short of expectations. In other cases, lesser modification may be required, but it is sensible to keep the project under regular review. In this area the investment appraisal system should partly merge with the management accounting/information system, which is designed to produce information for this type of use.

The opportunities for post-acceptance review will vary greatly with the type of project and type of company. At one extreme might be a retailing organisation which opens several dozen new stores each year. Past experience can generate sophisticated models to predict store traffic and other factors, and these models can be improved by checking new store performance against forecasts. Projected cash flows from new stores can be built into the company-wide cash forecasting system and variances can immediately be identified.

With one-off projects it is much harder to use post-acceptance analysis to improve future decisions. If a particular line of technical development of a product turns out to be a dead end, this may have little feedback value for other technical projects under consideration.

Most investment projects are inherently risky. When a project fails to live up to expectations, this does not mean that the investment appraisal process has failed, or that those who made the estimates should be blamed. It is very important that post-acceptance analysis does not degenerate into a hunt for scapegoats. Good working relationships and mutual trust within the organisation are, in the last resort, the best defence against unrealistic and over-optimistic forecasts.

3. The third criticism is that modern investment appraisal techniques reflect an opportunistic approach to company management which scans widely for money-making opportunities and moves the company to take advantage of them. It is a characteristic business method of the shapeless conglomerate, often employed by corporate planning staff who are removed from direct experience of operations. By dissipating the firm's energies into a variety of high-return, unrelated projects, the steady development of the company's core strengths in technology, marketing and other areas is neglected. The lack of a long-term corporate perspective gives investment decision-making a bias towards short-term, fast payback projects. This criticism is more widely heard in the US than in the UK. British experience of large conglomerate enterprises such as Hanson and BTR has been more favourable than American experience.

An alternative approach would put strategic factors first. This would start with an analysis of the strengths *vis-à-vis* competitors that the company has or expects to develop in the long run. Weakness of a long-term nature must also be identified. Projects are then chosen which fall within the company's area of competitive advantage. The advantages of a clear sense of strategic direction are that investments are likely to be mutually reinforcing, benefiting from shared technology and distribution arrangements, and that projects are likely to follow on from one another. When one project terminates the company is likely to be able to continue to employ many of the same skills and resources. Finally, a company can make better estimates of costs, demand, etc. if it stays within its area of expertise than if it ventures outside.

Is an investment programme strongly constrained by strategic considerations likely to make less money than one with fewer constraints? Not necessarily. The search for high-yield investments is very much limited by the workings of competitive markets. Over short periods there will always be parts of the economy which are over-supplied, so that returns are low, and others that look very exciting because they are undersupplied. These situations are temporary. One of the main functions of a free economy will be to move resources into areas of undersupply, and when this has been done profits will go back to normal levels. Events can move quickly, and the danger for a company that sets its investment trawl too wide is that it will be continually changing direction and puffing and panting towards profit opportunities which tend, like mirages, to disappear as soon as they come close. It is well worth asking, for any major investment project, 'What advantages do we have in this market compared to potential competitors?' If there are no relative advantages, and, even worse, if there are disadvantages, then there must be some doubt about forecast cash flows that show a superior investment return.

Conclusion

This book has concerned itself mainly with project definition and appraisal calculations. It has tried to cover both these topics in sufficient detail to be useful to professional financial analysts. It has limited its discussion of appraisal theory to areas where theory can be readily translated into practice.

Project appraisal is a large subject. Project definition has required a fairly detailed discussion of the UK fiscal system so that tax effects can be incorporated correctly. Appraisal calculations have included the basic material on NPV and IRR but have gone on to demonstrate methods of risk analysis and the special approaches that are needed for lease evaluation, replacement decisions and other topics. Some of the material is uncontroversial. In other areas there are a number of rival methods. Several different techniques have been explained for calculating the required rate of return for a project.

The variety of techniques and the large number of worked examples may seem confusing. It would be very unfortunate if the calculations attracted attention away from the underlying principles. The purpose of business investment is to increase shareholders' wealth. The different methods are all oriented towards this one objective. There is no one right way of making appraisals and this text is not intended to be a recipe book with exact instructions for every situation. Out of many acceptable methods of investment appraisal, this book has focused on one particular method, taking care to offer a consistent and logical treatment. There are a number of valid ways of defining cash flows and there are a number of valid ways of establishing a required rate of return, but the choice of method for measuring cash flow will require that the required return be selected on a compatible basis. We have tried to bring out these options because there are good reasons why one company may want to use a different appraisal system from another. A small company may want to use a simplified technique, such as WACC, which avoids detailed calculation of future taxes; a financially constrained company may want to use a capital rationing model; a hi-technology company in electronics or pharmaceuticals may want to put in specific forecasts of the trend of future product prices and costs; a public utility may prefer to assume that its prices and costs are more predictable in real than nominal terms and to do its calculations in purchasing power units as a result.

For a large project, a report should state prominently the key assumptions of revenues, costs, growth rates and other variables which are the basis of the cash flow forecasts. Some justification of the figures may well be needed. The calculations that follow are only as valid as the assumptions on which they are based. Discussions of a project's merits should centre on these assumptions. The technical merits of different types of appraisal calculation should be secondary. As long as those who use the figures understand them, there is no harm in including several different appraisal measures — IRR, NPV, payback or whatever — in the analysis. They may all be helpful to those making the final decision. We have already stressed the value of risk analysis. Sensitivity analysis, in particular, is always useful where there is uncertainty about the cash flow projections.

It may seem from this that, while others provide the creative input, the financial analyst just pushes the computer buttons. That is not true. Quite apart from the skill involved in presenting a clear and comprehensive report on a project, the analyst may be able to suggest ways in which a project might be modified to make it financially more attractive.

The basis of any project is a potentially money-making idea. The best way to develop the idea may not be immediately obvious. On what scale should the company invest initially? Should it seek a partner to share the risk and the reward? Is the project more attractive if assets are rented rather than bought? The basic idea behind a project is a block of marble which requires a lot of skilled work to produce the finished sculpture. Professional financial skills, along with other business skills, are needed to do the work.

Project appraisal, then, is a broad and diverse discipline. There are many different types of project, and many different types of company. There is also a wide variety, a smorgasbord, of different appraisal methods from which the analyst can choose. Bon appétit!

References and Further Reading

Hayes, R.H. and Garvin, D.A. (1982) 'Managing as if tomorrow mattered', *Harvard Business Review*, May–June, pp. 70–9.

King, P. (1975) 'Is the emphasis of capital budgeting theory misplaced?'. *Journal of Business, Finance and Accounting*, Vol. 12, No. 1, pp. 68–82.

Mao, J.C.T. (1970) 'Survey of capital budgeting: theory and practice', *Journal of Finance*, May, Vol. 25, No. 2, pp. 349–60.

Pike, R.H. (1982) *Capital Budgeting in the 1980s* I.C.M.A. Occasional Paper Series.

Pike, R.H. and Wolfe, M.B. (1987) *A Review of Capital Investment Trends in Large Companies*, University of Bradford Management Centre, Occasional Paper No. 8701/8702.

Appendix
Interest Rate Tables

Table 1   Amount of 1 at compound interest: $(1 + r)^n$

Years (n)	Interest rates (r) 1	2	3	4	5	6	7
1	1.0100	1.0200	1.0300	1.0400	1.0500	1.0600	1.0700
2	1.0201	1.0404	1.0609	1.0816	1.1025	1.1236	1.1449
3	1.0303	1.0612	1.0927	1.1249	1.1576	1.1910	1.2250
4	1.0406	1.0824	1.1255	1.1699	1.2155	1.2625	1.3108
5	1.0510	1.1041	1.1593	1.2167	1.2763	1.3382	1.4026
6	1.0615	1.1262	1.1941	1.2653	1.3401	1.4185	1.5007
7	1.0721	1.1487	1.2299	1.3159	1.4071	1.5036	1.6058
8	1.0829	1.1717	1.2668	1.3686	1.4775	1.5938	1.7182
9	1.0937	1.1951	1.3048	1.4233	1.5513	1.6895	1.8385
10	1.1046	1.2190	1.3439	1.4802	1.6289	1.7908	1.9672
11	1.1157	1.2434	1.3842	1.5395	1.7103	1.8983	2.1049
12	1.1268	1.2682	1.4258	1.6010	1.7959	2.0122	2.2522
13	1.1381	1.2936	1.4685	1.6651	1.8856	2.1329	2.4098
14	1.1495	1.3195	1.5126	1.7317	1.9799	2.2609	2.5785
15	1.1610	1.3459	1.5580	1.8009	2.0789	2.3966	2.7590
16	1.1726	1.3728	1.6047	1.8730	2.1829	2.5404	2.9522
17	1.1843	1.4002	1.6528	1.9479	2.2920	2.6928	3.1588
18	1.1961	1.4282	1.7024	2.0258	2.4066	2.8543	3.3799
19	1.2081	1.4568	1.7535	2.1068	2.5270	3.0256	3.6165
20	1.2202	1.4859	1.8061	2.1911	2.6533	3.2071	3.8697
25	1.2824	1.6406	2.0938	2.6658	3.3864	4.2919	5.4274

8	9	10	11	12	13	14	15	
1.0800	1.0900	1.1000	1.1100	1.1200	1.1300	1.1400	1.1500	1
1.1664	1.1881	1.2100	1.2321	1.2544	1.2769	1.2996	1.3225	2
1.2597	1.2950	1.3310	1.3676	1.4049	1.4429	1.4815	1.5209	3
1.3605	1.4116	1.4641	1.5181	1.5735	1.6305	1.6890	1.7490	4
1.4693	1.5386	1.6105	1.6851	1.7623	1.8424	1.9254	2.0114	5
1.5869	1.6771	1.7716	1.8704	1.9738	2.0820	2.1950	2.3131	6
1.7138	1.8280	1.9487	2.0762	2.2107	2.3526	2.5023	2.6600	7
1.8509	1.9926	2.1436	2.3045	2.4760	2.6584	2.8526	3.0590	8
1.9990	2.1719	2.3579	2.5580	2.7731	3.0040	3.2519	3.5179	9
2.1589	2.3674	2.5937	2.8394	3.1058	3.3946	3.7072	4.0456	10
2.3316	2.5804	2.8531	3.1518	3.4785	3.8359	4.2262	4.6524	11
2.5182	2.8127	3.1384	3.4985	3.8960	4.3345	4.8179	5.3503	12
2.7196	3.0658	3.4523	3.8833	4.3635	4.8980	5.4924	6.1528	13
2.9372	3.3417	3.7975	4.3104	4.8871	5.5348	6.2613	7.0757	14
3.1722	3.6425	4.1772	4.7846	5.4736	6.2543	7.1379	8.1371	15
3.4259	3.9703	4.5950	5.3109	6.1304	7.0673	8.1372	9.3576	16
3.7000	4.3276	5.0545	5.8951	6.8660	7.9861	9.2765	10.7613	17
3.9960	4.7171	5.5599	6.5436	7.6900	9.0243	10.5752	12.3755	18
4.3157	5.1417	6.1159	7.2633	8.6128	10.1974	12.0557	14.2318	19
4.6610	5.6044	6.7275	8.0623	9.6463	11.5231	13.7435	16.3665	20
6.8485	8.6231	10.8347	13.5855	17.0001	21.2305	26.4619	32.9190	25

Table 1 *(Continued)*

	16	17	18	19	20	21	22	23
1	1.1600	1.1700	1.1800	1.1900	1.2000	1.2100	1.2200	1.2300
2	1.3456	1.3689	1.3924	1.4161	1.4400	1.4641	1.4884	1.5129
3	1.5609	1.6016	1.6430	1.6852	1.7280	1.7716	1.8158	1.8609
4	1.8106	1.8739	1.9388	2.0053	2.0736	2.1436	2.2153	2.2889
5	2.1003	2.1924	2.2878	2.3864	2.4883	2.5937	2.7027	2.8153
6	2.4364	2.5652	2.6996	2.8398	2.9860	3.1384	3.2973	3.4628
7	2.8262	3.0012	3.1855	3.3793	3.5832	3.7975	4.0227	4.2593
8	3.2784	3.5115	3.7589	4.0214	4.2998	4.5950	4.9077	5.2389
9	3.8030	4.1084	4.4355	4.7854	5.1598	5.5599	5.9874	6.4439
10	4.4114	4.8068	5.2338	5.6947	6.1917	6.7275	7.3046	7.9259
11	5.1173	5.6240	6.1759	6.7767	7.4301	8.1403	8.9117	9.7489
12	5.9360	6.5801	7.2876	8.0642	8.9161	9.8497	10.8722	11.9912
13	6.8858	7.6987	8.5994	9.5964	10.6993	11.9182	13.2641	14.7491
14	7.9875	9.0075	10.1472	11.4198	12.8392	14.4210	16.1822	18.1414
15	9.2655	10.5387	11.9737	13.5895	15.4070	17.4494	19.7423	22.3140
16	10.7480	12.3303	14.1290	16.1715	18.4884	21.1138	24.0856	27.4462
17	12.4677	14.4265	16.6722	19.2441	22.1861	25.5477	29.3844	33.7588
18	14.4625	16.8790	19.6733	22.9005	26.6233	30.9127	35.8490	41.5233
19	16.7765	19.7484	23.2144	27.2516	31.9480	37.4043	43.7358	51.0737
20	19.4608	23.1056	27.3930	32.4294	38.3376	45.2593	53.3576	62.8206
25	40.8742	50.6578	62.6686	77.3881	95.3962	117.3909	144.2101	176.8593

24	25	26	27	28	29	30	
1.2400	1.2500	1.2600	1.2700	1.2800	1.2900	1.3000	1
1.5376	1.5625	1.5876	1.6129	1.6384	1.6641	1.6900	2
1.9066	1.9531	2.0004	2.0484	2.0972	2.1467	2.1970	3
2.3642	2.4414	2.5205	2.6014	2.6844	2.7692	2.8561	4
2.9316	3.0518	3.1758	3.3038	3.4360	3.5723	3.7129	5
3.6352	3.8147	4.0015	4.1959	4.3980	4.6083	4.8268	6
4.5077	4.7684	5.0419	5.3288	5.6295	5.9447	6.2749	7
5.5895	5.9605	6.3528	6.7675	7.2058	7.6686	8.1573	8
6.9310	7.4506	8.0045	8.5948	9.2234	9.8925	10.6045	9
8.5944	9.3132	10.0857	10.9153	11.8059	12.7614	13.7858	10
10.6571	11.6415	12.7080	13.8625	15.1116	16.4622	17.9216	11
13.2148	14.5519	16.0120	17.6053	19.3428	21.2362	23.2981	12
16.3863	18.1899	20.1752	22.3588	24.7588	27.3947	30.2875	13
20.3191	22.7374	25.4207	28.3957	31.6913	35.3391	39.3738	14
25.1956	28.4217	32.0301	36.0625	40.5648	45.5875	51.1859	15
31.2426	35.5271	40.3579	45.7994	51.9230	58.8079	66.5417	16
38.7408	44.4089	50.8510	58.1652	66.4614	75.8621	86.5042	17
48.0386	55.5112	64.0722	73.8698	85.0706	97.8622	112.4554	18
59.5679	69.3889	80.7310	93.8147	108.8904	126.2422	146.1920	19
73.8641	86.7362	101.7211	119.1446	139.3797	162.8524	190.0496	20
216.5420	264.6978	323.0454	393.6344	478.9049	581.7585	705.6410	25

Table 2 Present value of 1 at compound interest: $(1 + r)^{-n}$

Years (n)	Interest rates (r) 1	2	3	4	5	6	7	8
1	0.9901	0.9804	0.9709	0.9615	0.9524	0.9434	0.9346	0.9259
2	0.9803	0.9612	0.9426	0.9246	0.9070	0.8900	0.8734	0.8573
3	0.9706	0.9423	0.9151	0.8890	0.8638	0.8396	0.8163	0.7938
4	0.9610	0.9238	0.8885	0.8548	0.8227	0.7921	0.7629	0.7350
5	0.9515	0.9057	0.8626	0.8219	0.7835	0.7473	0.7130	0.6806
6	0.9420	0.8880	0.8375	0.7903	0.7462	0.7050	0.6663	0.6302
7	0.9327	0.8706	0.8131	0.7599	0.7107	0.6651	0.6227	0.5835
8	0.9235	0.8535	0.7894	0.7307	0.6768	0.6274	0.5820	0.5403
9	0.9143	0.8368	0.7664	0.7026	0.6446	0.5919	0.5439	0.5002
10	0.9053	0.8203	0.7441	0.6756	0.6139	0.5584	0.5083	0.4632
11	0.8963	0.8043	0.7224	0.6496	0.5847	0.5268	0.4751	0.4289
12	0.8874	0.7885	0.7014	0.6246	0.5568	0.4970	0.4440	0.3971
13	0.8787	0.7730	0.6810	0.6006	0.5303	0.4688	0.4150	0.3677
14	0.8700	0.7579	0.6611	0.5775	0.5051	0.4423	0.3878	0.3405
15	0.8613	0.7430	0.6419	0.5553	0.4810	0.4173	0.3624	0.3152
16	0.8528	0.7284	0.6232	0.5339	0.4581	0.3936	0.3387	0.2919
17	0.8444	0.7142	0.6050	0.5134	0.4363	0.3714	0.3166	0.2703
18	0.8360	0.7002	0.5874	0.4936	0.4155	0.3503	0.2959	0.2502
19	0.8277	0.6864	0.5703	0.4746	0.3957	0.3305	0.2765	0.2317
20	0.8195	0.6730	0.5537	0.4564	0.3769	0.3118	0.2584	0.2145
25	0.7795	0.6095	0.4776	0.3751	0.2953	0.2330	0.1842	0.1460
30	0.7419	0.5521	0.4120	0.3083	0.2314	0.1741	0.1314	0.0994
35	0.7059	0.5000	0.3554	0.2534	0.1813	0.1301	0.0937	0.0676
40	0.6717	0.4529	0.3066	0.2083	0.1420	0.0972	0.0668	0.0460
45	0.6391	0.4102	0.2644	0.1712	0.1113	0.0727	0.0476	0.0313
50	0.6080	0.3715	0.2281	0.1407	0.0872	0.0543	0.0339	0.0213

9	10	11	12	13	14	15	
0.9174	0.9091	0.9009	0.8929	0.8850	0.8772	0.8696	1
0.8417	0.8264	0.8116	0.7972	0.7831	0.7695	0.7561	2
0.7722	0.7513	0.7312	0.7118	0.6931	0.6750	0.6575	3
0.7084	0.6830	0.6587	0.6355	0.6133	0.5921	0.5718	4
0.6499	0.6209	0.5935	0.5674	0.5428	0.5194	0.4972	5
0.5963	0.5645	0.5346	0.5066	0.4803	0.4556	0.4323	6
0.5470	0.5132	0.4817	0.4523	0.4251	0.3996	0.3759	7
0.5019	0.4665	0.4339	0.4039	0.3762	0.3506	0.3269	8
0.4604	0.4241	0.3909	0.3606	0.3329	0.3075	0.2843	9
0.4224	0.3855	0.3522	0.3220	0.2946	0.2697	0.2472	10
0.3875	0.3505	0.3173	0.2875	0.2607	0.2366	0.2149	11
0.3555	0.3186	0.2858	0.2567	0.2307	0.2076	0.1869	12
0.3262	0.2897	0.2575	0.2292	0.2042	0.1821	0.1625	13
0.2992	0.2633	0.2320	0.2046	0.1807	0.1597	0.1413	14
0.2745	0.2394	0.2090	0.1827	0.1599	0.1401	0.1229	15
0.2519	0.2176	0.1883	0.1631	0.1415	0.1229	0.1069	16
0.2311	0.1978	0.1696	0.1456	0.1252	0.1078	0.0929	17
0.2120	0.1799	0.1528	0.1300	0.1108	0.0946	0.0808	18
0.1945	0.1635	0.1377	0.1161	0.0981	0.0829	0.0703	19
0.1784	0.1486	0.1240	0.1037	0.0868	0.0728	0.0611	20
0.1160	0.0923	0.0736	0.0588	0.0471	0.0378	0.0304	25
0.0754	0.0573	0.0437	0.0334	0.0256	0.0196	0.0151	30
0.0490	0.0356	0.0259	0.0189	0.0139	0.0102	0.0075	35
0.0318	0.0221	0.0154	0.0107	0.0075	0.0053	0.0037	40
0.0207	0.0137	0.0091	0.0061	0.0041	0.0027	0.0019	45
0.0134	0.0085	0.0054	0.0035	0.0022	0.0014	0.0009	50

Table 2 (Continued)

	16	17	18	19	20	21	22	23
1	0.8621	0.8547	0.8475	0.8403	0.8333	0.8264	0.8197	0.8130
2	0.7432	0.7305	0.7182	0.7062	0.6944	0.6830	0.6719	0.6610
3	0.6407	0.6244	0.6086	0.5934	0.5787	0.5645	0.5507	0.5374
4	0.5523	0.5337	0.5158	0.4987	0.4823	0.4665	0.4514	0.4369
5	0.4761	0.4561	0.4371	0.4190	0.4019	0.3855	0.3700	0.3552
6	0.4104	0.3898	0.3704	0.3521	0.3349	0.3186	0.3033	0.2888
7	0.3538	0.3332	0.3139	0.2959	0.2791	0.2633	0.2486	0.2348
8	0.3050	0.2848	0.2660	0.2487	0.2326	0.2176	0.2038	0.1909
9	0.2630	0.2434	0.2255	0.2090	0.1938	0.1799	0.1670	0.1552
10	0.2267	0.2080	0.1911	0.1756	0.1615	0.1486	0.1369	0.1262
11	0.1954	0.1778	0.1619	0.1476	0.1346	0.1228	0.1122	0.1026
12	0.1685	0.1520	0.1372	0.1240	0.1122	0.1015	0.0920	0.0834
13	0.1452	0.1299	0.1163	0.1042	0.0935	0.0839	0.0754	0.0678
14	0.1252	0.1110	0.0985	0.0876	0.0779	0.0693	0.0618	0.0551
15	0.1079	0.0949	0.0835	0.0736	0.0649	0.0573	0.0507	0.0448
16	0.0930	0.0811	0.0708	0.0618	0.0541	0.0474	0.0415	0.0364
17	0.0802	0.0693	0.0600	0.0520	0.0451	0.0391	0.0340	0.0296
18	0.0691	0.0592	0.0508	0.0437	0.0376	0.0323	0.0279	0.0241
19	0.0596	0.0506	0.0431	0.0367	0.0313	0.0267	0.0229	0.0196
20	0.0514	0.0433	0.0365	0.0308	0.0261	0.0221	0.0187	0.0159
25	0.0245	0.0197	0.0160	0.0129	0.0105	0.0085	0.0069	0.0057
30	0.0116	0.0090	0.0070	0.0054	0.0042	0.0033	0.0026	0.0020
35	0.0055	0.0041	0.0030	0.0023	0.0017	0.0013	0.0009	0.0007
40	0.0026	0.0019	0.0013	0.0010	0.0007	0.0005	0.0004	0.0003
45	0.0013	0.0009	0.0006	0.0004	0.0003	0.0002	0.0001	0.0001
50	0.0006	0.0004	0.0003	0.0002	0.0001	0.0001	0.0000	0.0000

24	25	26	27	28	29	30	
0.8065	0.8000	0.7937	0.7874	0.7812	0.7752	0.7692	1
0.6504	0.6400	0.6299	0.6200	0.6104	0.6009	0.5917	2
0.5245	0.5120	0.4999	0.4882	0.4768	0.4658	0.4552	3
0.4230	0.4096	0.3968	0.3844	0.3725	0.3611	0.3501	4
0.3411	0.3277	0.3149	0.3027	0.2910	0.2799	0.2693	5
0.2751	0.2621	0.2499	0.2383	0.2274	0.2170	0.2072	6
0.2218	0.2097	0.1983	0.1877	0.1776	0.1682	0.1594	7
0.1789	0.1678	0.1574	0.1478	0.1388	0.1304	0.1226	8
0.1443	0.1342	0.1249	0.1164	0.1084	0.1011	0.0943	9
0.1164	0.1074	0.0992	0.0916	0.0847	0.0784	0.0725	10
0.0938	0.0859	0.0787	0.0721	0.0662	0.0607	0.0558	11
0.0757	0.0687	0.0625	0.0568	0.0517	0.0471	0.0429	12
0.0610	0.0550	0.0496	0.0447	0.0404	0.0365	0.0330	13
0.0492	0.0440	0.0393	0.0352	0.0316	0.0283	0.0254	14
0.0397	0.0352	0.0312	0.0277	0.0247	0.0219	0.0195	15
0.0320	0.0281	0.0248	0.0218	0.0193	0.0170	0.0150	16
0.0258	0.0225	0.0197	0.0172	0.0150	0.0132	0.0116	17
0.0208	0.0180	0.0156	0.0135	0.0118	0.0102	0.0089	18
0.0168	0.0144	0.0124	0.0107	0.0092	0.0079	0.0068	19
0.0135	0.0115	0.0098	0.0084	0.0072	0.0061	0.0053	20
0.0046	0.0038	0.0031	0.0025	0.0021	0.0017	0.0014	25
0.0016	0.0012	0.0010	0.0008	0.0006	0.0005	0.0004	30
0.0005	0.0004	0.0003	0.0002	0.0002	0.0001	0.0001	35
0.0002	0.0001	0.0001	0.0001	0.0001	0.0000	0.0000	45
0.0001	0.0000	0.0000	0.0000	0.0000	0.0000	0.0000	45
0.0000	0.0000	0.0000	0.0000	0.0000	0.0000	0.0000	50

Table 3   Present value of an annuity of 1: $\dfrac{1 - (1 + r)^{-n}}{r}$

Years (n)	Interest rates (r) 1	2	3	4	5	6	7
1	0.9901	0.9804	0.9709	0.9615	0.9524	0.9434	0.9346
2	1.9704	1.9416	1.9135	1.8861	1.8594	1.8334	1.8080
3	2.9410	2.8839	2.8286	2.7751	2.7232	2.6730	2.6243
4	3.9020	3.8077	3.7171	3.6299	3.5460	3.4651	3.3872
5	4.8534	4.7135	4.5797	4.4518	4.3295	4.2124	4.1002
6	5.7955	5.6014	5.4172	5.2421	5.0757	4.9173	4.7665
7	6.7282	6.4720	6.2303	6.0021	5.7864	5.5824	5.3893
8	7.6517	7.3255	7.0197	6.7327	6.4632	6.2098	5.9713
9	8.5660	8.1622	7.7861	7.4353	7.1078	6.8017	6.5152
10	9.4713	8.9826	8.5302	8.1109	7.7217	7.3601	7.0236
11	10.3676	9.7868	9.2526	8.7605	8.3064	7.8869	7.4987
12	11.2551	10.5753	9.9540	9.3851	8.8633	8.3838	7.9427
13	12.1337	11.3484	10.6350	9.9856	9.3936	8.8527	8.3577
14	13.0037	12.1062	11.2961	10.5631	9.8986	9.2950	8.7455
15	13.8651	12.8493	11.9379	11.1184	10.3797	9.7122	9.1079
16	14.7179	13.5777	12.5611	11.6523	10.8378	10.1059	9.4466
17	15.5623	14.2919	13.1661	12.1657	11.2741	10.4773	9.7632
18	16.3983	14.9920	13.7535	12.6593	11.6896	10.8276	10.0591
19	17.2260	15.6785	14.3238	13.1339	12.0853	11.1581	10.3356
20	18.0456	16.3514	14.8775	13.5903	12.4622	11.4699	10.5940
25	22.0232	19.5235	17.4131	15.6221	14.0939	12.7834	11.6536
30	25.8077	22.3965	19.6004	17.2920	15.3725	13.7648	12.4090
35	29.4086	24.9986	21.4872	18.6646	16.3742	14.4982	12.9477
40	32.8347	27.3555	23.1148	19.7928	17.1591	15.0463	13.3317
45	36.0945	29.4902	24.5187	20.7200	17.7741	15.4558	13.6055
50	39.1961	31.4236	25.7298	21.4822	18.2559	15.7619	13.8007

8	9	10	11	12	13	14	15	
0.9259	0.9174	0.9091	0.9009	0.8929	0.8850	0.8772	0.8696	1
1.7833	1.7591	1.7355	1.7125	1.6901	1.6681	1.6467	1.6257	2
2.5771	2.5313	2.4869	2.4437	2.4018	2.3612	2.3216	2.2832	3
3.3121	3.2397	3.1699	3.1024	3.0373	2.9745	2.9137	2.8550	4
3.9927	3.8897	3.7908	3.6959	3.6048	3.5172	3.4331	3.3522	5
4.6229	4.4859	4.3553	4.2305	4.1114	3.9975	3.8887	3.7845	6
5.2064	5.0330	4.8684	4.7122	4.5638	4.4226	4.2883	4.1604	7
5.7466	5.5348	5.3349	5.1461	4.9676	4.7988	4.6389	4.4873	8
6.2469	5.9952	5.7590	5.5370	5.3282	5.1317	4.9464	4.7716	9
6.7101	6.4177	6.1446	5.8892	5.6502	5.4262	5.2161	5.0188	10
7.1390	6.8052	6.4951	6.2065	5.9377	5.6869	5.4527	5.2337	11
7.5361	7.1607	6.8137	6.4924	6.1944	5.9176	5.6603	5.4206	12
7.9038	7.4869	7.1034	6.7499	6.4235	6.1218	5.8424	5.5831	13
8.2442	7.7862	7.3667	6.9819	6.6282	6.3025	6.0021	5.7245	14
8.5595	8.0607	7.6061	7.1909	6.8109	6.4624	6.1422	5.8474	15
8.8514	8.3126	7.8237	7.3792	6.9740	6.6039	6.2651	5.9542	16
9.1216	8.5436	8.0216	7.5488	7.1196	6.7291	6.3729	6.0472	17
9.3719	8.7556	8.2014	7.7016	7.2497	6.8399	6.4674	6.1280	18
9.6036	8.9501	8.3649	7.8393	7.3658	6.9380	6.5504	6.1982	19
9.8181	9.1285	8.5136	7.9633	7.4694	7.0248	6.6231	6.2593	20
10.6748	9.8226	9.0770	8.4217	7.8431	7.3300	6.8729	6.4641	25
11.2578	10.2737	9.4269	8.6938	8.0552	7.4957	7.0027	6.5660	30
11.6546	10.5668	9.6442	8.8552	8.1755	7.5856	7.0700	6.6166	35
11.9246	10.7574	9.7791	8.9511	8.2438	7.6344	7.1050	6.6418	40
12.1084	10.8812	9.8628	9.0079	8.2825	7.6609	7.1232	6.6543	45
12.2335	10.9617	9.9148	9.0417	8.3045	7.6752	7.1327	6.6605	50

Table 3 (*Continued*)

	16	17	18	19	20	21	22	23
1	0.8621	0.8547	0.8475	0.8403	0.8333	0.8264	0.8197	0.8130
2	1.6052	1.5852	1.5656	1.5465	1.5278	1.5095	1.4915	1.4740
3	2.2459	2.2096	2.1743	2.1399	2.1065	2.0739	2.0422	2.0114
4	2.7982	2.7432	2.6901	2.6386	2.5887	2.5404	2.4936	2.4483
5	3.2743	3.1993	3.1272	3.0576	2.9906	2.9260	2.8636	2.8035
6	3.6847	3.5892	3.4976	3.4098	3.3255	3.2446	3.1669	3.0923
7	4.0386	3.9224	3.8115	3.7057	3.6046	3.5079	3.4155	3.3270
8	4.3436	4.2072	4.0776	3.9544	3.8372	3.7256	3.6193	3.5179
9	4.6065	4.4506	4.3030	4.1633	4.0310	3.9054	3.7863	3.6731
10	4.8332	4.6586	4.4941	4.3389	4.1925	4.0541	3.9232	3.7993
11	5.0286	4.8364	4.6560	4.4865	4.3271	4.1769	4.0354	3.9018
12	5.1971	4.9884	4.7932	4.6105	4.4392	4.2784	4.1274	3.9852
13	5.3423	5.1183	4.9095	4.7147	4.5327	4.3624	4.2028	4.0530
14	5.4675	5.2293	5.0081	4.8023	4.6106	4.4317	4.2646	4.1082
15	5.5755	5.3242	5.0916	4.8759	4.6755	4.4890	4.3152	4.1530
16	5.6685	5.4053	5.1624	4.9377	4.7296	4.5364	4.3567	4.1894
17	5.7487	5.4746	5,2223	4.9897	4.7746	4.5755	4.3908	4.2190
18	5.8178	5.5339	5.2732	5.0333	4.8122	4.6079	4.4187	4.2431
19	5.8775	5.5845	5.3162	5.0700	4.8435	4.6346	4.4415	4.2627
20	5.9288	5.6278	5.3527	5.1009	4.8696	4.6567	4.4603	4.2786
25	6.0971	5.7662	5.4669	5.1951	4.9476	4.7213	4.5139	4.3232
30	6.1772	5.8294	5.5168	5.2347	4.9789	4.7463	4.5338	4.3391
35	6.2153	5.8582	5.5386	5.2512	4.9915	4.7559	4.5411	4.3447
40	6.2335	5.8713	5.5482	5.2582	4.9966	4.7596	4.5439	4.3467
45	6.2421	5.8773	5.5523	5.2611	4.9986	4.7610	4.5449	4.3474
50	6.2463	5.8801	5.5541	5.2623	4.9995	4.7616	4.5452	4.3477

24	25	26	27	28	29	30	
0.8065	0.8000	0.7937	0.7874	0.7812	0.7752	0.7692	1
1.4568	1.4400	1.4235	1.4074	1.3916	1.3761	1.3609	2
1.9813	1.9520	1.9234	1.8956	1.8684	1.8420	1.8161	3
2.4043	2.3616	2.3202	2.2800	2.2410	2.2031	2.1662	4
2.7454	2.6893	2.6351	2.5827	2.5320	2.4830	2.4356	5
3.0205	2.9514	2.8850	2.8210	2.7594	2.7000	2.6427	6
3.2423	3.1611	3.0833	3.0087	2.9370	2.8682	2.8021	7
3.4212	3.3289	3.2407	3.1564	3.0758	2.9986	2.9247	8
3.5655	3.4631	3.3657	3.2728	3.1842	3.0997	3.0190	9
3.6819	3.5705	3.4648	3.3644	3.2689	3.1781	3.0915	10
3.7757	3.6564	3.5435	3.4365	3.3351	3.2388	3.1473	11
3.8514	3.7251	3.6059	3.4933	3.3868	3.2859	3.1903	12
3.9124	3.7801	3.6555	3.5381	3.4272	3.3224	3.2233	13
3.9616	3.8241	3.6949	3.5733	3.4587	3.3507	3.2487	14
4.0013	3.8593	3.7261	3.6010	3.4834	3.3726	3.2682	15
4.0333	3.8874	3.7509	3.6228	3.5026	3.3896	3.2832	16
4.0591	3.9099	3.7705	3.6400	3.5177	3.4028	3.2948	17
4.0799	3.9279	3.7861	3.6536	3.5294	3.4130	3.3037	18
4.0967	3.9424	3.7985	3.6642	3.5386	3.4210	3.3105	19
4.1103	3.9539	3.8083	3.6726	3.5458	3.4271	3.3158	20
4.1474	3.9849	3.8342	3.6943	3.5640	3.4423	3.3286	25
4.1601	3.9950	3.8424	3.7009	3.5693	3.4466	3.3321	30
4.1644	3.9984	3.8450	3.7028	3.5708	3.4478	3.3330	35
4.1659	3.9995	3.8458	3.7034	3.5712	3.4481	3.3332	40
4.1664	3.9998	3.8460	3.7036	3.5714	3.4482	3.3333	45
4.1666	3.9999	3.8461	3.7037	3.5714	3.4483	3.3333	50

Table 4 Terminal value of an annuity of 1: $\dfrac{(1 + r)^n - 1}{r}$

Years (n)	Interest rates (r)							
	1	2	3	4	5	6	7	8
1	1.0000	1.0000	1.0000	1.0000	1.0000	1.0000	1.0000	1.0000
2	2.0100	2.0200	2.0300	2.0400	2.0500	2.0600	2.0700	2.0800
3	3.0301	3.0604	3.0909	3.1216	3.1525	3.1836	3.2149	3.2464
4	4.0604	4.1216	4.1836	4.2464	4.3101	4.3746	4.4399	4.5061
5	5.1010	5.2040	5.3091	5.4163	5.5256	5.6371	5.7507	5.8666
6	6.1520	6.3081	6.4684	6.6330	6.8019	6.9753	7.1533	7.3359
7	7.2135	7.4343	7.6625	7.8983	8.1420	8.3938	8.6540	8.9228
8	8.2857	8.5830	8.8923	9.2142	9.5491	9.8975	10.2598	10.6366
9	9.3685	9.7546	10.1591	10.5828	11.0266	11.4913	11.9780	12.4876
10	10.4622	10.9497	11.4639	12.0061	12.5779	13.1808	13.8164	14.4866
11	11.5668	12.1687	12.8078	13.4864	14.2068	14.9716	15.7836	16.6455
12	12.6825	13.4121	14.1920	15.0258	15.9171	16.8699	17.8885	18.9771
13	13.8093	14.6803	15.6178	16.6268	17.7130	18.8821	20.1406	21.4953
14	14.9474	15.9739	17.0863	18.2919	19.5986	21.0151	22.5505	24.2149
15	16.0969	17.2934	18.5989	20.0236	21.5786	23.2760	25.1290	27.1521
16	17.2579	18.6393	20.1569	21.8245	23.6575	25.6725	27.8881	30.3243
17	18.4304	20.0121	21.7616	23.6975	25.8404	28.2129	30.8402	33.7502
18	19.6147	21.4123	23.4144	25.6454	28.1324	30.9057	33.9990	37.4502
19	20.8109	22.8406	25.1169	27.6712	30.5390	33.7600	37.3790	41.4463
20	22.0190	24.2974	26.8704	29.7781	33.0660	36.7856	40.9955	45.7620
25	28.2432	32.0303	36.4593	41.6459	47.7271	54.8645	63.2490	73.1059

9	10	11	12	13	14	15	
1.0000	1.0000	1.0000	1.0000	1.0000	1.0000	1.0000	1
2.0900	2.1000	2.1100	2.1200	2.1300	2.1400	2.1500	2
3.2781	3.3100	3.3421	3.3744	3.4069	3.4396	3.4725	3
4.5731	4.6410	4.7097	4.7793	4.8498	4.9211	4.9934	4
5.9847	6.1051	6.2278	6.3528	6.4803	6.6101	6.7424	5
7.5233	7.7156	7.9129	8.1152	8.3227	8.5355	8.7537	6
9.2004	9.4872	9.7833	10.0890	10.4047	10.7305	11.0668	7
11.0285	11.4359	11.8594	12.2997	12.7573	13.2328	13.7268	8
13.0210	13.5795	14.1640	14.7757	15.4157	16.0853	16.7858	9
15.1929	15.9374	16.7220	17.5487	18.4197	19.3373	20.3037	10
17.5603	18.5312	19.5614	20.6546	21.8143	23.0445	24.3493	11
20.1407	21.3843	22.7132	24.1331	25.6502	27.2707	29.0017	12
22.9534	24.5227	26.2116	28.0291	29.9847	32.0887	34.3519	13
26.0192	27.9750	30.0949	32.3926	34.8827	37.5811	40.5047	14
29.3609	31.7725	34.4054	37.2797	40.4175	43.8424	47.5804	15
33.0034	35.9497	39.1899	42.7533	46.6717	50.9804	55.7175	16
36.9737	40.5447	44.5008	48.8837	53.7391	59.1176	65.0751	17
41.3013	45.5992	50.3959	55.7497	61.7251	68.3941	75.8364	18
46.0185	51.1591	56.9395	63.4397	70.7494	78.9692	88.2118	19
51.1601	57.2750	64.2028	72.0524	80.9468	91.0249	102.4436	20
84.7009	98.3471	114.4133	133.3339	155.6196	181.8708	212.7930	25

Table 4 *(Continued)*

	16	17	18	19	20	21	22	23
1	1.0000	1.0000	1.0000	1.0000	1.0000	1.0000	1.0000	1.0000
2	2.1600	2.1700	2.1800	2.1900	2.2000	2.2100	2.2200	2.2300
3	3.5056	3.5389	3.5724	3.6061	3.6400	3.6741	3.7084	3.7429
4	5.0665	5.1405	5.2154	5.2913	5.3680	5.4457	5.5242	5.6038
5	6.8771	7.0144	7.1542	7.2966	7.4416	7.5892	7.7396	7.8926
6	8.9775	9.2068	9.4420	9.6830	9.9299	10.1830	10.4423	10.7079
7	11.4139	11.7720	12.1415	12.5227	12.9159	13.3214	13.7396	14.1708
8	14.2401	14.7733	15.3270	15.9020	16.4991	17.1189	17.7623	18.4300
9	17.5185	18.2847	19.0859	19.9234	20.7989	21.7139	22.6700	23.6690
10	21.3215	22.3931	23.5213	24.7089	25.9587	27.2738	28.6574	30.1128
11	25.7329	27.1999	28.7551	30.4035	32.1504	34.0013	35.9620	38.0388
12	30.8502	32.8239	34.9311	37.1802	39.5805	42.1416	44.8737	47.7877
13	36.7862	39.4040	42.2187	45.2445	48.4966	51.9913	55.7459	59.7788
14	43.6720	47.1027	50.8180	54.8409	59.1959	63.9095	69.0100	74.5280
15	51.6595	56.1101	60.9653	66.2607	72.0351	78.3305	85.1922	92.6694
16	60.9250	66.6488	72.9390	79.8502	87.4421	95.7799	104.9345	114.9834
17	71.6730	78.9792	87.0680	96.0218	105.9306	116.8937	129.0201	142.4295
18	84.1407	93.4056	103.7403	115.2659	128.1167	142.4413	158.4045	176.1883
19	98.6032	110.2846	123.4135	138.1664	154.7400	173.3540	194.2535	217.7116
20	115.3797	130.0329	146.6280	165.4180	186.6880	210.7584	237.9893	268.7853
25	249.2140	292.1049	342.6035	402.0425	471.9811	554.2422	650 9551	764.6054

24	25	26	27	28	29	30	
1.0000	1.0000	1.0000	1.0000	1.0000	1.0000	1.0000	1
2.2400	2.2500	2.2600	2.2700	2.2800	2:2900	2.3000	2
3.7776	3.8125	3.8476	3.8829	3.9184	3.9541	3.9900	3
5.6842	5.7656	5.8480	5.9313	6.0156	6.1008	6.1870	4
8.0484	8.2070	8.3684	8.5327	8.6999	8.8700	9.0431	5
10.9801	11.2588	11.5442	11.8366	12.1359	12.4423	12.7560	6
14.6153	15.0735	15.5458	16.0324	16.5339	17.0506	17.5828	7
19.1229	19.8419	20.5876	21.3612	22.1634	22.9953	23.8577	8
24.7125	25.8023	26.9404	28.1287	29.3692	30.6639	32.0150	9
31.6434	33.2529	34.9449	36.7235	38.5926	40.5564	42.6195	10
40.2379	42.5661	45.0306	47.6388	50.3985	53.3178	56.4053	11
50.8950	54.2077	57.7386	61.5013	65.5100	69.7800	74.3270	12
64.1097	68.7596	73.7506	79.1066	84.8529	91.0161	97.6250	13
80.4961	86.9495	93.9258	101.4654	109.6117	118.4108	127.9125	14
100.8151	109.6868	119.3465	129.8611	141.3029	153.7500	167.2863	15
126.0108	138.1085	151.3766	165.9236	181.8677	199.3374	218.4722	16
157.2534	173.6357	191.7345	211.7230	233.7907	258.1453	285.0139	17
195.9942	218.0446	242.5855	269.8882	300.2521	334.0074	371.5180	18
244.0328	273.5558	306.6577	343.7580	385.3227	431.8696	483.9734	19
303.6006	342.9447	387.3887	437.5726	494.2131	558.1118	630.1655	20
898.0916	1054.7912	1238.6363	1454.2014	1706.8031	2002.6156	2348.8033	25

Index